Worth Fighting For Series
Book 1: Orphans

^A BRUISED
Reed

Memoirs of
African Orphans and
Their Rescuers

ENDORSEMENTS

"If you have ever wondered why missionaries do what they do in abandoning the comforts of home and blazing off to another continent, country, and culture, this book, *A Bruised Reed*, answers that: it's the children. Yes, of course there is the call of Jesus, but the children keep calling to them even across the ocean. I have trained nearly a thousand missionaries and have contact presently with hundreds more, but I have never heard or read a more compelling story than this one lived out by my friends Tracy and Becky Spencer."

—John T. Hollar, Director Emeritus
Christ For The Nations Institute

"A Bruised Reed is a book that will capture your heart and challenge your spirit. Becky takes us into the lives and homes of orphans from Swaziland, reminding us that God often expresses His love and care through us. We cannot ignore the needs of those around us, whether near or far, because all are precious in God's sight. These pages brim with the hope of transformation and the honesty of hardship and heartache. You cannot help but be encouraged, challenged, and inspired."

—Eric Wilson, NY Times bestselling author of
Fireproof, October Baby, and *Samson*

"In 2017 I was privileged to accompany Becky and her husband Tracy to Swaziland. There I embraced Vamsile. As her American sponsor, I heard her gratitude for the privilege of learning at a Christian school. Like Vamsile, my heart was filled with love and gratitude for Becky and Tracy, seeing first-hand their embrace of unloved, abandoned, and needy Swazi children. My life was changed. Yours will be, too, by this heart-felt memoir of a ministry in Swaziland that is, undeniably, on the move, with miracle stories between its covers that will move your faith to new heights. I will read *A Bruised Reed* more than once, and so will you as you are stirred to obedience to the Bible."

—Steve Rees, freelance Christian journalist

"'Some people look at the suffering around the world and ask why a good God would allow it,' Becky writes. 'But He is asking why *we* allow it. He is willing and deeply desires that the needs are met. But He uses people.' God is definitely using Becky and Tracy Spencer to make a difference. He will use you, too, in ways beyond what you can ask or imagine, if you'll let Him. This book can change your life!"

—Marlene Bagnull, Author, Speaker, Editor
Director of Write His Answer Ministries
Colorado Christian Writers Conference
Greater Philly Christian Writers Conference
Publisher of Ampelos Press

"Because I'm well acquainted with Becky's zeal for God, passion for others (especially the Swaziland orphans), and ability to bring beauty to ugly situations, I knew before I even read a word of this book that I would be uplifted and inspired. What I didn't expect is how Becky's words and these stories would jolt me out of my everyday petty frustrations and open a broad vista of hope in light of the "bigger picture." Sure, the Lord could intervene supernaturally in the lives of hurting children, but He takes pleasure in working through His followers to provide the human touch. Thank you, Becky and Tracy, for heeding the Father's call and making it possible for the rest of us to be a part of this vital ministry. Your example of compassion and faithfulness provide a needed boost and 'reality check' for us all."

"Get ready to go on a missions trip! Not a physical journey—although you might be moved to join Becky Spencer or another of God's anointed and directed overseas ministers after you read *A Bruised Reed*. But this book is a 'trip' all by itself, the record of heartfelt burdens and lovingkindness for those who hurt and are vulnerable; of amazing breakthroughs, entering into lands and facing challenges with no possible ideas of what lies ahead; of teachers, ministers, role models, empty vessels, and yielded saints. And souls who are hurt, lonely, sick, and needing Christ. Many of us have contact with missions only via annual fund appeals, or neighborhood kids on two-week projects. We might read letters sharing great victories or see videos of agonizing crises. But *A Bruised Reed* is a trip beyond any of that – Becky's accounts of real needs, real triumphs; of real trust and sometimes real betrayals; of steps of faith and unimaginable miracles. All in places you probably never heard of and might not ever visit, except for the gift of this telling. What a trip!"

A BRUISED *Reed*

Memoirs of African Orphans and Their Rescuers

Becky Yates Spencer
"The Fight Lady"

Grand Staff
PUBLISHING

A Bruised Reed: Memoirs of African Orphans and Their Rescuers

"Worth Fighting For" series, Book 1: Orphans

Copyright © 2018 by Becky Yates Spencer

Published by Grand Staff Publishing
PO Box 321
Buhler KS 67522
(620) 543-6518
www.grandstaffministries.com

ISBN 0-9747561-4-8

Cover design by Cathy Sanders
cathysanders.design@gmail.com

Edited by Marlene Bagnull and Barbara Haley

Typeset by Barbara Haley

Unless otherwise noted, Scripture quotations taken from the Amplified® Bible, Classic Edition (AMPC), Copyright © 1954, 1958, 1962, 1964, 1965, 1987 by The Lockman Foundation. Used by permission. www.Lockman.org

Scripture quotations taken from AMPLIFIED Bible, Copyright © 1954, 1958, 1962, 1964, 1965, 1987, 2015 by The Lockman Foundation. All rights reserved. Used by permission. (www.Lockman.org)

Song "Will You Save Me?" copyright © 2012 Anna (Spencer) Harper, used by permission.

Song "If You Could See Them Like I See Them" copyright © 2010 Becky Spencer.

Song "Well Done" copyright © 2005 Becky Spencer.

Some of the names of our Swazi children and others have been changed to protect their identities.

We acknowledge that earlier this year the king of Swaziland, King Mswati III, changed the name of the kingdom to eSwatini. Since it means "land of the Swazi's in the local language, siSwati, in this book we will use the English translation, which remains Swaziland.

Printed in the United States of America

DEDICATION

This book is dedicated to our Men of Courage.

Before I wrote this book, I only had a skeleton idea of what you endured. You opened your hearts and your mouths to flesh that out, filling in the missing pieces as you answered my many questions. With great courage, you have lived up to your name.

I know you bore your souls in hopes that other children will be spared some of the pain you went through. May this be the case as others read and weep and act.

For every one of you who gave expression to your sorrows, may you experience healing.

You are heard. You are believed. And you no longer have to bear your burden alone. To those of you whose pain was still too raw to voice it, we will be here for you when you're ready.

Papa Tracy and I care. You know many others love you, too. Soon a vast army of godly believers will also stand with you.

May the Lord Jesus make a beautiful melody with your lives.

Mama Becky

A bruised reed He will not break, and a dimly burning wick He will not quench; He will bring forth justice in truth.

Isaiah 42:3

Table of Contents

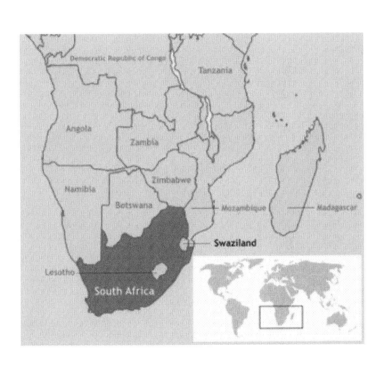

FOREWORD

Her stories broke my heart as she gave vulnerable children in Swaziland, Africa, a voice. I first heard Becky when she introduced Grand Staff Ministries with a power point presentation at a writing conference. As the images of hurting Swazi children pierced me, the Holy Spirit immediately filled me with God's love for these Swazi orphans and Grand Staff Ministries. Perhaps because I, myself, have been called by God to minister to children.

Many years ago I took a college entrance exam. The counselor said, "Your test results are amazing. I'd suggest you pursue engineering. It's a lucrative career and your mathematical scores are over the top."

Despite her counsel, I became an elementary teacher. At that time in my life I had three young children. I still wanted to be Mommy—not an overworked accountant or engineer.

Ten years later, though, I stopped to ponder that choice. If I'd gone into engineering, our lives would have looked so different in terms of wealth and status.

But as my weak flesh wobbled, God reminded me of why I'd made my choice. My biological children. And then, His children. The students I'd taught for many years.

The Bible makes it clear how dearly God loves children. As I thought about that, I realized how very honored I was to be asked to minister to God's babies. Never again would the desire for more money come close to my love and appreciation for serving God in this way.

Fast forward thirty years. My kids are raised. God has blessed me above and beyond in so many ways that I am now able to pour into the ministry, the Swazi children's lives, financially.

Tracy and Becky Spencer are two of the most compassionate, wise, and courageous people I know. And let's add OBEDIENT. I'm so thankful Becky wrote these stories—but telling them isn't enough. Each story is a cry for help that still fills me with a longing to be part of the answer. The needs have shocked me out of my comfortable lifestyle to a point where I will never again take all that I have for granted. God has called me to action. He has called me to pray. And He has called me to give sacrificially to these children.

I pray that as you read these stories, you will also stop and meditate. Take a moment to put yourself in each child's life. Own that child's fears, hopelessness, hunger, and pain. Pray with fervency for each child.

Then make a commitment. Think sacrificially.

I once read that LOVE is making a peanut butter sandwich for a kiddo. But *LOVINGKINDNESS* is adding the jelly.

What can you do ... TODAY?

In Christ's love,

Barbara E. Haley
Author of *Biz On the Go* and *Lord, Get Your Needle—I'm Falling Apart at the Seams*
Universal City, Texas

"Let us not become weary in doing good, for at the proper time we will reap a harvest if we do not give up" (Galatians 6:9 NIV).

Acknowledgements

Okay, I admit that I've never conducted the scientific research on this. But I would guess that at least 75% of Americans answer the question, "How are you?" with the reply, "Busy!"

It's the American way, isn't it? Even with our modern conveniences to make tasks easier, we're rushing most of the time and feel like we'll never catch up with our to-do lists.

I'm no different. Early in March, during a week intended to be a restful Sabbatical, I felt the call to write this book. I scratched out a tentative rough draft, easy enough to do when I had no other pressing duties.

But I went home to the busiest season of our ministry. I'd just caught my breath from five weeks of mission work in Swaziland, Africa. Our annual fundraiser was seven weeks away. And it was time for me to return to my regular work schedule at our ministry thrift boutique.

It seemed like the worst possible time to take on a book project. But God seems to love the word "impossible." Apparently, He also loves *me*, because He sent His faithful followers to come alongside to help, even with their own busy schedules.

Steve Rees, I think Encourager must be your middle name. Every word that comes out of your mouth and through your pen lifts me up. Thank you for sponsoring Vamsile, for writing articles about Grand Staff Ministries, for praying faithfully for Tracy and me, for going with us to Swaziland, and for speaking life into my writing, even on those days when I've wondered if I've lost my mind and missed God altogether. You only had a small window of time on the weekend to read the manuscript, but you set aside your other responsibilities so you could give me feedback. (I still say we should all call you Barnabas.)

Hope Flinchbaugh, you are more than an author, more than an editor, more than a mentor. The first time I saw you across the Ruesch Auditorium at the Colorado Christian Writer's Conference, I knew we would be friends. I simply had to know you. We discovered so many shared callings—singer/songwriters, adoptive mothers, and staunch warriors for hurting children all over the world. Mike Wolff got it right when he dubbed us the "Sisters of Thunder." But God knew we were destined to shake things up from our unique personalities. While I push ahead like a steam roller, you sit at the tree of life and wait on the Lord. Thank you for advising me to catch my breath and forget my self-imposed deadline. You insisted that I let the stories of the children come alive and dance, and you reminded me how to do it. Thank you, my sweet sister, for helping me slow down so I could keep pace with the Holy Spirit—and for "loaning" Cathy to us to make the cover sing.

Rick Marschall, when I dove into this book, you were sailing high in your own research for a book that is sure to have great historical significance. Besides which, you had your regular writing jobs, including your stint as Editor-in-Chief of *Michigan Innovative Health Magazine*, blogging on your weekly *Monday Morning Music Ministry*, a comeback as Editor to the soon-to-be-return of "Nemo," and whatever else you surely have on your plate to add to your nearly eighty books to your credit. I'm convinced you don't sleep. But you do make me belly laugh, and you took the time to send puns and funnies so I wouldn't abandon ship. The bonus was your advice about how to navigate the choppy waters of deadlines—even how to know when it's time to throw them overboard and let the boat float awhile. Thank you, Buddy. Your wit was a beacon for me.

Mama (Pattie Yates Belden), you have always been my greatest supporter. Well, that's not your only claim to fame.

You're also a dynamite speed reader. You zoomed through the manuscript in one afternoon, flourishing your yellow highlighting pen and convincing me the book needed just one more story about a child at the end. You also managed to make me believe that you honestly, for sure, positively would not be the only person in the world who would find the book worth reading. Thank you, Mama, for always believing, for putting in countless hours of sweat equity for this ministry, for running circles around women half your age to do that, for putting your money on the line for the children, and for being one of my best friends. Grand Staff Ministries wouldn't exist without you.

Marlene Bagnull, I've never met anyone more obviously called of God to connect people for His Kingdom purposes. From the first time I attended the Colorado Christian Writers Conference and ever since, I've been amazed by the selfless way you give a platform to people who are writing God's answer—to a hurting world and to the sometimes just-as-messy church. Thank you for inviting me to share our Swaziland mission at the Colorado conference and at the Greater Philadelphia Christian Writers Conference. Thanks for going the extra mile when I couldn't be in Philly—you and Barbie shared what Grand Staff Ministries is doing in Swaziland, and you were so effective, more offerings came in that day than in any other fundraising endeavor we've ever taken on. Because you gave this ministry a voice, many Swazi children have been sponsored so they could go to school, and our first care home was finished and opened its doors over a year ago.

On top of all of that, you've also jumped right in on this book project. You refused to let me give up when the timeline seemed too daunting. You gave me advice about countless options for the look and feel of the book. You insisted I stick with the Lord's leading and get the book written, no matter the obstacles. And talk about getting involved during a busy season—you've even edited the manuscript the week before the Philly conference! That's always a time of intense opposition from the evil one, and this time has been no different. Your computer has acted like it's demon-possessed, you've fallen, and you've got poison ivy! But you wouldn't take the way out I offered you out of concern for your well-being. Thank you for caring, for being patient with me, and for laying down your life for the least of these.

Barb Haley, I hardly even know where to begin when trying to list the ways you've helped me and Grand Staff Ministries. Long before this book was even a concept, you were already serving behind the scenes. You facilitate many aspects of the writers' conferences so we wordsmiths can learn and grow and fulfill God's call on our lives. You belt out your praise when we gather around the piano for worship and bless us when you take your turn tickling the ivories as we wind down from the Colorado conference every year. You're always ready to stop what you're doing to pray with everyone who has a need—and I've been blessed to be on the receiving end of those petitions to heaven. You donate profits from your own book sales to our mission work. You give from your financial resources in such a way that your late husband would be honored by your generosity.

You made sure I took a week off from my normal duties so I wouldn't burn completely out—and that time away is what got me quiet before the Lord long enough to hear His heart for the stories in this book to be told. You did extensive editing on this book, and you also formatted it for printing—even the week before the Philly conference while you helped Marlene prepare. Barbie, you are the epitome of a servant of the Lord, giving way past what's comfortable, all the way to where it's a sacrifice—a laying down of your life for the One Who saved you and now uses you to touch hearts for Him. Thank you for all you've done, including touching this heart of mine. I love you.

Janis Pauls, for the past six years, you have faithfully taken the load off my shoulders as you've stepped up as Grand Staff Ministries' auction coordinator. You handle the mailings so I can scoot off to Swaziland in January. You call every business owner, many of them more than twice. You track who's doing what and keep things organized. Like me, you have an amazing hubby, and Dennis, I know that you're the one who drives all over Kansas to pick up a couple hundred items and gift certificates. Then your daughter Abby and her husband Caleb Cooley get in on the action as your family completely sets up for the silent auction portion of the event. Even some of your grandchildren are now taking up the mantle! I don't have to give that part of the event a single thought, leaving me free to do other aspects of ministry without neglecting the fundraising that keeps things afloat. And an added bonus is that ever since you took this over, we've had increasingly excellent auctions! Thank you, my dear friends, for doing whatever it takes to get the job done. (Yep, guys, even picking up the stage too many times in a row!) Heaven sees, and so do I, with deep love.

Paula Wiens, God sent you to Grand Staff Ministries and the thrift boutique when we needed you most. There's no way I could've written this book without your faithful leadership at the store. And you covered for me even while your knees were screaming! You are so easy to work with, and even easier to love. The Lord knew it wasn't just GSM that needed you; He sent you to my heart, too, because I needed a friend. Bless you, bless you, bless you, sweet girl. And thank you. I don't know how I ever managed without you before. (We are long overdue for a Monday girl day, complete with massages and Mexican food and chocolate!)

If I tried to name everyone else who pitched in extra hours at Grand Staff Thrift Boutique so I could write—and every time I go to Swaziland—I'd never be able to mention everyone. You are the backbone of making the vision come to pass in the village, and only eternity will reveal how far-reaching your efforts have been. Every bag you've sorted through, every piece of clothing you've steamed, every customer you've checked out—each task reaches across the ocean and into the heart of a child. Oh, heaven is recording your labor of love for the Lord and His sweet little ones in Swaziland! And I thank you from the depths of my soul.

Thank you to everyone else who has supported the work in Swaziland, Africa. You have given financially, brought your gently-used treasures to the thrift boutique, and donated amazing items to the auctions. You have prayed for me, my family, our board of directors, our Swazi ministry partners, our sponsors, and the children of Swaziland. You've gone with me to Swaziland. You've sponsored children. Some of you I've never even met, but our Savior has seen everything you've done quietly, and He will reward you.

Thank you to every church, women's group, and organization that has invited me to share the mission God has called us to.

To everyone who has faithfully served on the Grand Staff Ministries Board of Directors, my heart runs over with appreciation. You've laid down your lives, sacrificing family time and resources to meet the needs of the kids. And you have patiently guided this ADD creative soul so the important tasks and decisions still get done—on time! Thank you doesn't begin to cover it.

Stan and Sue Drew, my precious friends and missionaries to Swaziland, you connected my heart to the children from the start. You have held me when my heart was breaking, advised me when the way forward was unclear, carefully corrected me when I needed an attitude adjustment, and inspired me by your example of compassionate service to our precious Swazi children. Although you never held a birth child in your arms, you have held countless brown-skinned children in your hearts, always making room for one more. Thank you, Papa Stan and Mama Sue. Swaziland is a better place because of your service there, and heaven is all the richer.

To my kids and grandkids, Jesus sees the times you've hoped I could visit or babysit or hang out with you, but I needed to work on something for this ministry. My precious loved ones, I know Jesus has made our times together even sweeter, because His whole Kingdom is built on finding our lives through laying them down. I believe He has special surprises waiting for you in heaven, and meanwhile, I'm sure thankful for the way He's blessing our family with incredible love while we're still on this side of glory, too. I love you all *this much!* (All the way up to heaven, down to the bottom of the sea, and way in the bottom of my heart!)

Tracy, my love, I'll never forget the day you wanted to talk to me about our first trip to Swaziland. You took my face in your hands and insisted I make eye contact with you. Then you lovingly looked deeply into my eyes and gently spoke from your heart. "Becky, we're not bringing any of the children home with us." Oh, honey, you know me so well! As has often the been the case, you were afraid I'd rush out ahead of you and leave you wondering what had happened. But look what Jesus has done. He's changed us over these past twelve years as we've sought justice for the children of Swaziland. You have faithfully partnered with me, using up your vacation days from work to go with me. You've become quite good at driving on the left side of the road, seated on the right. You've brought home countless meals from a drive through, not only during this current writing project, but also while we got the boutique up and running and I've been simply too tired to cook. You're my favorite Fix-it Man, my best friend, and the one I'm blessed to call my husband. Thank you for making my dreams your own and helping make these God-sized dreams come true.

Jesus, thank you for never breaking me when I was bruised. You're the best.

Introduction

When a duck lands on a reed in the marshland, the reed snaps. But when a man walks past and brushes the reed, it is bruised, seemingly useless. After all, with so many reeds available, why make a basket or a flute from a bruised reed? Just break it off and find a different one.

I can't think of any better description of the plight of our precious children in Swaziland, Africa.

Life in Swaziland is hard enough. The disease, poverty, and hunger press down, especially on the children.

But it's what adults have done to these children that has left them bruised, in body and in soul.

You will read about unthinkable deeds here—rape, abandonment, beatings, and forced servitude.

Even from family members.

Worse, you'll learn the ways many have suffered spiritual abuse from individuals who were supposed to share God's love with them. Souls crushed . . . hope extinguished.

Because there are so many children in Swaziland without an adult to care for them, exhausted social workers are often unmoved by the atrocities being committed against these kids. There aren't enough care homes to go around. Nor enough social workers.

So they listen to the stories, but before the ink is dry on their notes of one case, the phone is already ringing with the next crisis. Even though they care, their lack of action speaks the opposite to hurting kids.

But when Jesus sees these children, He has justice in His eyes. He would never do anything to further harm them. Though some would consider them too wounded to amount to anything, He insists that He is able to make something of what is left.

Something worthwhile. Something beautiful.

He has allowed my husband Tracy and me to have the honor of bringing His love and hope to many of these beautiful chocolate-skinned children.

Countless people have joined us to bring justice to the kids. The task is not over.

Most of you will never cross the ocean to hold these little ones in your arms. But it is my hope that as you turn these pages, you will experience God's immeasurable love for Swaziland's children. If our heavenly Daddy carries a wallet in the pocket of His robes, He surely has a picture of every one of these kids in it, right beside His pictures of you and me and our children and grandchildren—we are all that dear to His heart! Let me introduce you to Jabu, and you will see why.

The Call

Jabu

Way back when I was five years old, my parents got into a conflict. This turned out to be one of the worst days of my life. I stood meters away, watching my dad beating my mother. My mom had serious injuries, especially in the head.

The next morning, she took me and my younger brother to our grandmother's place. This was a sign that my dad and mom were divorcing. We stayed at Grandma's most of that year. But two men came and said to both Mom and Grandma, "As you can see and hear us, we are sent by the father of these children to come and take them home with us."

We didn't want to leave our mother. We loved her so much, because she was the one who took care of us. At first, she didn't want to hand us to these men, but finally she packed our things and let them take us. She even accompanied us halfway to the bus station. When she turned to go, we couldn't hold ourselves back from crying. She wished us a safe journey, and we left.

The first person we saw when we entered our dad's house was a lady. He later told us to give full respect to her and to listen to everything she told us to do. He added that we should forget our mom, because we had a new mother now.

This woman called us bad names. "You are stupid. You are a fool." She accused us of stealing things we hadn't taken.

Sometimes she forced us to do heavy tasks too hard for our ages, like fetching water in big containers for long distances. We also had to grind mealy meal and cook it. If these things were not carried out in time, she beat us severely. We were told that it was a life lesson.

One day my stepmom told me to go to the kitchen to get a knife. I asked her what for, and she said she wanted to kill my brother for urinating in bed during the night. Thanks be to God, she didn't kill him, but he was beaten severely hard that morning. Another time she burned him in the kitchen for wetting his bed. But somehow she didn't succeed in murdering him.

Still, her abuse of my brother continued. On one really bad day for him, when she kept him trapped in our room, my brother was clever enough to pour water on the stick and mud wall until it was wet. He pushed it and found his way out. When school was out that day, I found him seated by the school gate, and we both went home. That's when he shared with me how he'd escaped. Both of us were beaten hard that day.

On another instance, when I came home from school, I found my brother lying in bed. I said to him, "You look unhappy; what's wrong today, brother?" He did not answer my question, but took his left hand out. I could not believe what I saw. I was shocked and terrified, stricken with pain. I asked him what had happened to him, and he said, "Mother did this to me. She took my hand forcefully and put it in boiling water, because I had urinated in bed last night." His hand was full of blisters, and I could tell he was in pain because he was not treated. This left me without anything to say.

The stepmom kept abusing us till things were worse. Near the end of the year 2000, when I was six years old, she used a sharp object to stab my brother right on top of where the kidneys are. She then hid that sore, and it was damaged so badly that it became swollen. It took some time before it was healed.

My brother got attacked by a sickness; none of us knew what it was. He was rushed to the hospital and admitted. He stayed in the hospital for over a month and then was discharged. While he was in the hospital, I stayed at a neighbor's place. Even there, life was not pleasant.

When my brother got better and seemed fine, his illness started again. This time, after less than a month in the hospital, he died. He was only three years old.

One day as I was searching through some documents back at our house, I came across a paper with information showing how my brother died: it was due to food poisoning. I knew it was done by my stepmom.

This whole thing left me still without anything to say, but I felt a great pain. Even today when I think of that, I still feel that pain, simply because I loved my brother. We both depended on each other for our happiness. In those days, if ever I could show a smile, it was because of my brother, and if he did, I was the one responsible for that. "May your soul rest in peace, brother."

Early the morning of his brother's funeral, Jabu was told to pack all his things. It took him only minutes to wad up his meager belongings. There were police at the funeral, and they didn't allow him to return home. After tearing himself away from his final goodbye to his little brother, the superintendent of his school drove him quite a distance, where he stayed three days with a pastor and his family. From there he was taken to Challenge Ministries, where he met Pastor Kevin Ward, a good man from the UK who has served in Swaziland for decades.

Upon investigation, it was discovered that Jabu was covered in sores all over his body and needed treatment for the frequent, severe beatings he'd received from his stepmother. He was given clothes and toys, then was taken to Pastor Luendo's church to stay. Jabu became part of a family with the other guys who had been given refuge there. Fear of going back home caused Jabu to be on his best behavior at his new home so there would be no reason for him to be sent away.

Life changed completely for him. He experienced love. He had clothes, shoes, toiletries, and he ate until he was satisfied. He enjoyed playing soccer, going to school, and attending church. For the first time, he felt like he belonged.

From the author:

In my wildest dreams, I never imagined meeting Jabu. I wasn't one of those people who grew up knowing I would be a missionary.

In fact, I fantasized about being a star. My playtime was spent being the lead singer in my own do-wop band, using Grandma Yates's plastic banana for a microphone. My sisters and cousins were the background singers to Grandma's 45 vinyl records. We acted out "Walk Right In," practiced our dance moves to "The Twist," and crooned the lyrics to "Downtown."

Other times I pretended to be a teacher, lining up my younger siblings to spell my dictated words or figure the addition and subtraction problems I wrote out for them.

But I never dreamed about service in another country. And I sure didn't consider myself "Africa material."

God did.

And He knew exactly where to find me—at a yard sale in the United States! As they say, "One man's trash is another man's treasure." And while I had my eye on discovering great bargains on some of those treasures, God's eye was on Jabu, the treasure of His heart.

God's Call to Africa— From a Yard Sale!

In June of 2003, Tracy and I and our four youngest children traveled from our home in Kansas to Seattle, Washington. We were visiting our dear family friends, Ron and Coleen Yocum, and attending the high school graduation of their daughter Jubilee.

While driving through the Yocum's neighborhood, we saw signs for yard sales all over the place, and even furniture offered for free by the curbs. Tracy and I decided to go bargain hunting on Saturday morning.

He pulled up to the curb at our first house. I hurried out of the car, eager to start filling the back of our Suburban with great finds. I made a beeline for a colorful globe on the first table. Tracy was slower in his approach, ambling up the sidewalk and engaging Stan, the homeowner, in conversation.

As I grabbed the globe, balanced some white glass containers with lids in the other hand, and carefully added sharp steak knives to the top of the stack, I overheard bits and pieces of their conversation. When Stan mentioned "South Africa," he got my attention. I walked to the checkout table and unloaded my finds, eager to join the discussion.

Stan's wife, Sue, welcomed me with her friendly smile, and they each shook my hand as I introduced myself as Tracy's wife. I guessed them to be in their mid-fifties, still vibrant with their obvious love for God and orphans. They took turns describing their assignment in Swaziland, Africa, explaining that they were selling their few belongings they'd accumulated during their fund-raising furlough. Both had a contagious enthusiasm for their mission to vulnerable children suffering from the AIDS crisis in that part of the world.

My enthusiasm bubbled to the surface as I sensed God had orchestrated our meeting. I explained that we were from Kansas, visiting Seattle for Jubilee's graduation. I explained that she was leaving for South Africa that summer to study with Youth with a Mission for ten months—and that our son Benjamin was also going to South Africa for a month that summer on a mission trip with Global Expeditions. Then I asked if they thought they could talk to the kids about what to expect.

Their smiles grew even bigger as they quickly agreed to explain the culture to Jubilee and Ben and give them advice about what to take with them on their journeys. Sue and I scribbled our contact information on scraps of notebook paper and exchanged them with each other, promising to connect after graduation.

Tracy pulled out some cash to pay for our purchases, and we left the Drew's with a warm sense of God's goodness. Out of the hundreds of rummage sales in Seattle that morning, even with our total ignorance of the neighborhoods, He had guided us to this particular home.

Stan and Sue made good on their promise to give helpful information to the teenagers. We'd made a nice acquaintance. We were done, right?

Well, not quite. When Tracy and I got back to our home in Kansas, we couldn't quit thinking about this couple. We love missions and have supported lots of missionaries through the years, but never someone we didn't really know outside of our denomination. Yet we felt compelled to be a small part of the Drew's ministry. So, for about fifteen years, we've been honored to sow financially into their service in Swaziland.

But the Lord wasn't done even then. Over the next couple of years, we stayed in touch with Stan and Sue through email messages. Stan eventually relayed his side of the story about the day we'd met them at their rummage sale. He said, "When I looked at our meager offering of items, I knew it would never get us to Swaziland. So I joined hands with Sue while we prayed for divine appointments all day."

Tracy and I were their first customers of the day, sent by God for His eternal purposes—astounding since we weren't praying specifically for any big spiritual encounter. We were just looking for good deals!

Naturally, neither did we have any idea at that time that God's plan went beyond using Tracy and me as part of the answer to Stan and Sue's prayers. He also planned all along to use them as part of the answer to our prayers about what our next assignment would be since six of our eight children were now adults.

The only way I know to describe what happened next is that both Tracy and I started to feel "pulled" to Swaziland.

There was no lightning. No thunder. No voice from heaven. Only this sense of being drawn.

Now remember: I. Didn't. Consider. Myself. Africa. Material.

All I could picture about a stint in Africa was oppressive heat, monster-sized bugs, and poisonous snakes. No thanks!

But the pull wouldn't go away.

One weekend in 2005 I spent a couple of days with our son Benjamin, who by then was an intern with Teen Mania Ministries in east Texas. On Saturday, we lounged in our hotel room. Ben was sprawled sideways across his bedspread, his blonde hair messy and falling across his forehead. I faced him from my seat on the edge of my bed, enjoying our easy conversation as we caught up on what had been happening in his life since our last visit.

I wanted to catch him up on our latest news, too. I filled him in on what was happening with his seven siblings and their families and updated all the news about our mutual church friends.

But my tone changed as I got to the more serious issues we were considering. "Ben, will you please pray about something for Daddy and me? You know that with most of you kids grown up now, we've been wondering what God wants us to do next. Justin only has one more year of high school left, and Anna's already in third grade. I love homeschooling them, but it seems like the Lord might have something more for us to do."

I described what his dad and I were both feeling when we thought about Swaziland, also offering the reasons why I was hesitant to take it too seriously.

Ben cocked his head sideways as he grew thoughtful. When his blue eyes met mine, he gently exhorted me with these words: "Mom, don't you think we pray a long time about things God already said to do? He already told us to go into all the world and make disciples."

My eyes widened as he continued with greater passion. "But then we don't pray about things we should pray about, like whether or not to watch that movie or what to wear."

I was stunned at the simplicity he'd nailed by stripping down our questions and excuses to the pure truth of Jesus' command.

When I got back home, I relayed this conversation to Tracy. We joked about our son. When had Ben gotten to be so smart? But we also marveled at the wisdom of his words.

Then I went to my office to open my email. (Yes, back then you had to do it on your computer.)

I had a message waiting from Stan, asking me when we were coming to Swaziland.

What? I hadn't said anything to Stan and Sue about traveling over there!

I called Tracy to join me, and he leaned over the back of my chair to follow along the computer screen as I read Stan's email to him. As we faced each other and grabbed hands to pray, tears came to my eyes. We acknowledged the obvious. We didn't need to seek the Lord for any further confirmation that He was calling us to go. Rather, we needed to start raising our funds.

Since we had absolutely no idea what God had in mind for us, we determined we should stay in Swaziland for one month. Our Anna was only ten years old, and I couldn't imagine leaving her for that long. Also, if we were going to end up living in Swaziland long-term, we wanted her to experience the culture with us. We decided to take her with us.

We had more questions about our future than answers, but we were willing to do whatever He wanted us to do.

First, though, we needed to raise $10,000.

The interesting thing about raising money is that even before we met Stan and Sue, Tracy and I had been praying for direction about what the Lord wanted us to do next. For about three years, everywhere we turned, we were hearing messages about finances. Turn on Christian radio: money. Sermons at church: money (which was rare at the church we attended). Christian television: money.

Even one weekend when Tracy and I had gotten away for our anniversary, the Lord continued to show us Scriptures about money. We didn't go looking for them—they were just in our regular readings for that Saturday morning. We weren't even in the same place in our Bibles. But after we had our personal devotions, we came back to share with each other, and once again both of us had been impressed with Scriptures about money.

We chuckled as we wrote down the passages and thoughts in our notebooks. Even teased that the Lord might have the wrong house as He kept sending messages about money. After all, Tracy is a machinist. I was then mostly staying at home and educating our two youngest children. With eight kids, we had never been people with a lot of money.

But we sensed the Lord wanted us to understand how He operates in that realm. And we realized that it was an important topic, because Jesus spoke more about money than He spoke about heaven!

During that time, one morning I was suddenly awake. It was exactly 3:00 a.m. I wasn't dreaming when I "heard" these words clearly: "Money is only a resource."

I sat up in my bed and grabbed the notebook and pen I keep handy in case I get an idea for a song or book. This time I knew I wasn't being creative; this was a message from the Lord. I quickly scribbled down the words from God and waited attentively.

The rest of the message produced awe in my heart: "It's nothing more, and it's nothing less. I'm calling you to some things that will take a lot of it, but that won't be your concern. My resources are unlimited. I created the universes out of nothing."

When I was sure that was the end of the message, I raised my hands in surrender to whatever the Lord wanted to do in us and through us. It was still a mystery, but He was getting us ready.

And honestly, I wasn't sure exactly how the call to go to Swaziland fit with whatever God had in mind for us regarding money, other than the expense of making the trip. So we prayed over the need, then got busy.

Thinking often of how we'd met Stan and Sue, we held our own rummage sales. We sent out support letters. We prayed a lot. And we booked our flights to coincide with a team from Dallas/Fort Worth that was also going on a mission trip to Swaziland during our scheduled visit in June/July of 2006.

Departure day finally arrived. It was a Sunday morning, and we went to church first. We were packed up and ready to head south to the DFW Airport to meet up with the Texas team. But we were still short a few hundred dollars. With only hours until departure, what could we do? We loaded up our van and pulled out of our driveway in faith.

After service, our church had a going-away lunch for us. As friends and family hugged us and said their goodbyes, various people pressed bills into our hands. After we got buckled up and drove away, we counted up the bills.

We had exactly the amount we needed.

And we were off on our adventure with God to see why He was asking us to make this trip.

He didn't disappoint us.

Part of His why became obvious through Colani's story.

Colani, Street Kid

I know what it's like to be hungry.

My parents and grandparents died, and I was living in the streets of Mbabane, the capital of Swaziland. I was not quite seven years old.

Each day was spent trying to get food. There was no fun. No games. No baths. No tooth-brushing. No school.

I stayed together with five other little boys. They became like a family to me. We all shared whatever we had—food, clothing given to one of us by a Good Samaritan, money. All six of us shared one blanket. I can still remember curling up into a tight ball so I wouldn't use up more than my share of the blanket during the cold nights.

We relieved ourselves in bushes around town since we had no toilet.

We also slept in bushes around town. At one point, we managed to put together a little shack from cardboard, plastic, and wood. But when it rained, the primitive hut provided no shelter. We had to walk into the downtown area, where we hid in the shop verandas. Night security guards treated us like garbage, berating us for being in town during late hours and beating us.

In the mornings, we would split up to increase our chances of someone finding piece jobs to do to try to get some food. On good days, I could convince a vendor on the street to allow me to carry large crates of produce, sweep the sidewalk, or do other jobs in exchange for one piece of fruit.

Sometimes I stole food from street vendors. I would pretend I was just passing by, but I was really eyeing the food to make a plan about what I could quickly take. Maybe a piece of fruit or a vegetable, maybe a King's pie pastry, or maybe even an ear of maize roasting over a slow fire. As soon as I thought the vendor wasn't paying attention, I would grab the food and run away with it as quickly as I could.

At first, my heart would beat fast and my hands would sweat with the fear of being caught. But soon it became a big challenge to get away with the theft. If the vendor caught me, I was beaten. The punishment was worth the food. I never felt guilty. I was so hungry and had no one to take care of me.

Every so often, the police caught me stealing or running from the vendors. When they did, they also beat me. They took me to the police station. To punish me, they forced me to work very hard. I became bitter toward them because they were so quick to make me pay for what I'd done wrong, but they never gave me any life solution for my situation.

When my friends and I met up late in the day, we compared what we'd collected and split up the food. Even on the days we ate, we were hungry again in a few hours.

I can still remember the smells of the dust bins [trash cans] in town. Rotting cabbages, filthy nappies [baby diapers], potato peelings caked with dirt—they were horrible. But the other boys and I still took turns climbing into the dumpsters, making steps out of our joined hands to boost each other up high enough to make it over the top. Then we'd dig around for anything edible, even the food that had decayed, because our bellies complained with pain. Being picky was a luxury we couldn't afford.

Some vendors became fond of me. I learned to sweet talk them out of their damaged fruits, using my sad eyes and rubbing my belly to show how desperate I was for some sustenance. I even used my smile to move them, because at first, they might resist helping me, but they couldn't help smiling back at me when I turned on my charm.

It didn't work on everyone, and it didn't work every day. But it worked often enough to become one of my regular acts.

It just seemed like I could never get full.

Occasionally some stranger would see my need and give me some food or some money for food.

When nothing else worked and we boys couldn't find or steal food, we all went to sleep with empty stomachs.

The best day I remember from my days in the streets was when a stranger gave me E200; I felt like a very rich boy, because I was able to buy food to share with the other five boys. The emalangeni [Swazi money] was the equivalent of about $20.

Christmas isn't a happy time for a child living in the streets. I only remember celebrating one time. Some Nigerians took me off the street to their hotel where they made me take a shower. They brought out some clothes I was allowed to keep, fed me, and wished me a Merry Christmas. Their kindness was a light to my soul.

But there were also dark times.

Sometimes people would beat me and my friends in the streets. Men also tried to sodomize me and the other guys. I learned to run very fast. One of the five boys was caught by a man who succeeded in sodomizing him. The boy received injuries from the attack, but we couldn't take him to the doctor. The sores got infected, and he ran a fever. He died a few weeks later.

Losing my "brother" was the saddest experience of my life.

One of my worst memories is something that happened to me personally. It was winter, and I was downtown looking for bread or potato chips late at night. I was distracted by the sound of a tire blowing out, resulting in the driver running into the car in front of him.

After watching a few minutes, I heard a man calling to me to come across the street. Since I was used to begging for food and money, I wasn't concerned; I hoped to receive some help from this man.

As I neared his car, he told me he had some clothes for me in his boot [trunk]. I smiled and moved closer. Very few people were downtown at that time of night, and those gathered were still watching the scene of the accident.

The man opened the boot, but instead of pulling out clothes for me, he grabbed me by the arms and dragged me quickly across the rough pavement, injuring my back.

He bundled me up in the boot and drove away with me. I screamed loudly, but no one answered. I could hear other cars passing by and horns honking now and then. The smell of petrol burning pressed down on me, and the blanket wrapped around my face became damp from my breath.

I was terrified. My heart was a big lump in my throat, and after screaming so much, I had trouble swallowing past the rawness. As we drove farther from town, I worried about my friends who would wonder where I was that night. I tried not to think about my family or if any aunts or uncles who were still living would ever know what happened to me.

Fear tortured me as we left the sounds of the city and traffic. When the car finally stopped, I heard the man slam his car door. The smell of cigarette smoke drifted into the boot, and I screamed again, gasping for air as my terror nearly suffocated me. But there was no one to hear my cries.

Finally, my abductor opened the trunk. He unwrapped the blanket from my squirming body, managing to keep his hold on me the whole time. When my head was freed from the blanket, I saw that he had a large knife in one hand. I knew he was going to murder me.

He dragged me out of the boot, using one hand to hold me and the other to keep his knife ready. When he told me to pull down my pants, I knew that what he planned to do to me would be worse than death.

My voice was raspy, nearly nothing left after screaming for so long. But I struggled to make noise and kept wrestling away as much as my shaking body allowed.

I don't know if I prayed, but suddenly the sound of his cell phone ringing cut through the night. While he juggled to answer it, I managed to bite him with all my strength. He lost his grip on me, and I took off running through the trees and bushes. He came after me, but all those years of running from the street vendors and police gave me an advantage. I outran him.

I had no idea where I was, but I kept running full speed. I fell into a deep ditch, further injuring my back and loosening my teeth. I stayed in the ditch the rest of the night, and when morning came, I walked until I found my way back into town.

My friends took me to the Salvation Army clinic, where my injuries were treated. They gave me medication to keep infection away.

Even now, more than twenty years later, my spine still hurts from the injuries I got that night when he dragged me away. Every time I feel the pain, I relive that memory, over and over, amazed that I survived. Even though I didn't know God at that time, He was still watching out for me.

Sadness took over my life. So many bad things were happening to all of us, I felt like giving up. Instead, I found ways to numb my pain. Sometimes when a kind person gave me money for food, I would find someone of legal age to buy me alcohol. I quickly reached a place of preferring the relief from the pain in my soul even more than the relief food gave for the pain in my belly.

Even though I had lived on the streets for six years, I was still just a child.

When I was thirteen years old, a kind stranger took me to live at Challenge Ministries. I should have been happy. I received food regularly. I had a narrow bed with a foam mattress to sleep on, out of the elements. But it was like a living hell to me. I wasn't used to being on a schedule or following a routine. I ran away from there, but eventually another Good Samaritan took me back again. I ended up being taken to a care home where I slowly made good friends with another group of boys who had suffered much like I had.

They would end up being more of a family to me than anyone else who had been in my life up to that point.

And we were going to need each other in the years to come more than we could have dreamed.

Colani's experiences were not isolated; thousands upon thousands of children in Swaziland also endured neglect, hunger, abuse, and fear.

Cold, hard facts about the HIV/AIDS pandemic painted a bleak picture. But God wanted us to see His desire to rescue children from the mistreatment that was breaking them. He wanted us to join our hearts to His—to let His compassion grow in us.

Our first trip to Swaziland helped us grasp the need behind the statistics, moving us to action so we could become part of His rescue effort for the children who were so much more than a number.

Why Swaziland?

June, 2006

God told me to fly across the ocean
Just to save that one little boy,
A boy who cried, "God, can you save me?"

Excerpt from "Will You Save Me?"

Tracy, ten-year-old Anna, and I landed in Johannesburg, South Africa, on a sunshiny morning after journeying for over thirty hours. Tracy was grateful that we were with a team from Dallas who were experienced travelers—we'd have been lost navigating through customs and baggage claim.

Stan and Sue with Becky and Tracy, 1ˢᵗ trip in 2006

Stan and Sue were a welcome sight just outside of security, and we embraced gratefully. They helped us exchange our US dollars into South African Rand, which would also be accepted in Swaziland. They'd brought a bus and driver for the rest of the twenty-two members of the team to ride in as we drove the four hours to Swaziland. But since our little family was staying longer, we needed to rent a car.

My emotions were fighting for preeminence. On one hand, I was eager to finally stand on the verge of finding out God's plans for us, but on the other, I was battling fear, distrust, and insecurity.

My first concern was for Anna. Her straight blonde hair bounced just below her ears, making her stand out in the crowded airport as she made eye contact with everyone around us. She'd never known a stranger, and I was worried that she'd run off with an unsavory character. Images of human trafficking crowded my mind, and I urged her to stand near me at all times, even keeping one hand on my arm to make sure we weren't separated.

I also feared the high prevalence of HIV/AIDS. What if one of us got raped? It would be horrifying in any culture, but in my mind, a possible death sentence here. I checked Anna's hands for any small cuts that might allow the disease entry into her little body. To be honest, I checked my own hands, as well, and Tracy's. Even though I'd done some research into the ways the virus could be contracted, I'm a bit of a germaphobe, and my active imagination had kicked into overdrive. I stuffed down my fear and tried to smile.

But I was exhausted, nervous that we'd lose the rest of the large group, overwhelmed by the smells of perspiration and jet fuel fumes. The many languages being spoken loudly in this international hub distracted me, and I needed to pay attention to Stan's instructions.

As we made our way out of the airport to the car rental area, sweaty dark men surrounded us like vultures, trying to take over our two lumbering luggage carts. They wanted to be paid for helping; Stan shooed them away.

We finally got the keys to our little Toyota Taz hatchback and managed to get a month's worth of luggage crammed into it. Tracy took a few minutes to adjust to sitting behind the steering wheel on the right side of the car, shifting the gears on his left, and driving on the opposite side of the streets. He managed to maneuver the car into place behind the team's bus, both of us shocked at how crowded the city was.

As we made our way out of Johannesburg, the countryside soothed our rattled nerves. That part of South Africa reminded us a lot of Kansas. The fields were flat and green, and we could almost imagine a farmer driving his John Deere tractor into the crops. But the scenery soon included little shanty towns, where stick and mud huts were situated close to each other. Colorful laundry was strung along fences and naked toddlers chased each other in the yards.

We all stopped at a convenience gas station about halfway to Swaziland and ordered lunch in the sit-down burger joint. Anna laughed with me that it was named "Steers," since my uncle raised cattle and talked about his head of steer. I figured it was better to laugh than to get grossed out at the reminder of what we were consuming. At least it wasn't monkey meat, as people has teased we'd be sampling. We were surprised that the beef tasted pretty much like home, even if the ketchup, or tomato sauce, as they call it in Africa, had lot more vinegar than ours and came out of the dispenser fast because it was so thin.

The closer we got to Swaziland, the more excited we became. The landscape became mountainous, and the people captivated our attention. Young mothers carried babies and toddlers swaddled onto their backs. Older women walked along the roads balancing tubs of water or bags of oranges on top of their heads, both hands also hefting large bags of beans or sugar or rice.

Men waved at us, smiling from the backs of open truck beds, too many crammed into the small space, some of them even standing precariously as they bumped along. Children of all ages walked along in their school uniforms, the greens and blues and plaids proudly identifying what school they belonged to. No one was in a hurry, except for the occasional hitchhiker running across the street to catch a ride.

Anticipation was winning the battle as the miles flew by. Who would we meet? What would we find? Where would God lead?

My nerves were taut again when we went through customs into Swaziland. Stan instructed us to explain to the authorities that we were there on "holiday," or vacation. He encouraged us to be calm and use soft voices as we answered questions. And he had already prayed that none of us would be held up with extensive inspections of our belongings.

We got through customs without incident and drove less than thirty minutes more past the border to reach Emafini, the Christian conference center where we were staying. The three of us had rented a delightful little cottage with a thatched roof. I was surprised by how clean it was. And how well stocked with towels and dishes for our use.

Although the windows had no screens, they allowed a cool breeze to circulate the air inside the small space. And I have to admit, the indoor flushing toilet was a huge relief—on our flight, I'd imagined we'd have to use an outhouse or squat in the bush.

Anna making friends with our maid, Esther, in front of our cottage

When everyone was rested, we were fascinated by the cultural training given by Pastor Kevin Ward, a native of the United Kingdom who has served in Swaziland for several decades. Although I'd read what I could find on the country, the information made more sense through his firsthand narrative:

- Swaziland is the last absolute monarchy in the world. The king, Mswati III, has reigned since 1986. There are about one million people in the kingdom.

- Surrounded by South Africa on the north, south, and west, and by Mozambique on the east, this beautiful country of cool mountains and hot, dry valleys is about the size of Vermont.
- The country is a polygamous society. Many times when a man brings home a second wife, the first one abandons the family for another man, leaving her kids with a woman who doesn't love them or want them. The sense of abandonment and rejection is overwhelming.
- Swaziland has the highest incidence of HIV/AIDS in the world. Because of the lowered immune defenses from that disease, they also have more tuberculosis than any other country.
- Almost 2/3 of all deaths in Swaziland are caused by HIV/AIDS. Almost half of all deaths of children five years and younger are caused by the disease. And more than 1/3 of tested pregnant women are HIV positive, leaving infants at high risk for the disease.
- Because of HIV/AIDS, Swaziland has the fourth lowest life expectancy in the world.
- Statistics on HIV/AIDS are based on those who actually get screened. However, a huge stigma remains, and many individuals haven't been screened. Experts there believe up to half the population has HIV/AIDS.

We also learned that experts predicted the country would be extinct by 2026. No other nation has ever survived with the ratio of children to adults Swaziland was experiencing. And that was downright eerie. During our trip, we met very few Swazis in their late 30s to early 50s. And even fewer grandpas.

All the statistics and information came alive, however, when we started interacting with Swazis.

The Government Hospital

One of our first stops was at the government hospital in the capital of Mbabane. Nothing Stan or Kevin told us could have prepared us for the dismal conditions. Even the halls reeked with urine, feces, blood, and perspiration.

The walls and floors were so filthy, I wished I'd had latex gloves for everyone to wear, especially Anna. I held her close when part of the team split off to go to the AIDS ward, while our little family joined the other part visiting the children's ward.

We quickly learned that a nurse's job in the government hospital is mostly to administer medications.

People aren't even admitted unless they can provide their own caregiver. There are no hospital meals on trays clattering down the hall to wake people up from their drug-induced slumber. No cheerful nurse aides popping in to fluff pillows or ask on a scale of one to ten, where the pain registers.

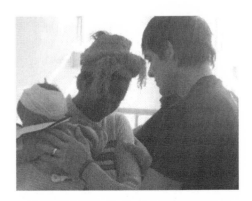

Instead, hopelessness reigns.

We split into groups of three to five, each group taking along one Swazi who could interpret for us when necessary. We took turns handing out candy and rolls, offering to pray for the sick children.

Young mothers who couldn't have been more than fifteen or sixteen years old were lethargic, many suffering from HIV/AIDS, and worse, the knowledge that they'd passed the virus on to their tiny babies.

Several older children were suffering from injuries sustained when they were hit by cars. We learned that this is common in Swaziland where most children walk to and from school. Open wounds oozed and festered while children moaned under dirty, threadbare blankets. It seemed everyone waited endlessly for someone in authority to show up and help. Many patients were in obvious agony.

I was shocked to find that the doctors and nurses offered no explanations to the caregivers or patients concerning diagnoses or planned treatment. These professionals considered questions an offense to their superior knowledge. Swazis are trained to go along with authority, never questioning decisions affecting them or their loved ones.

Stan quietly explained to us that there are only 2,000 hospital beds in Swaziland. My mind reeled with the implications. If half of the population in this kingdom of one million people was suffering with HIV/AIDS, then where did the remaining 498,000 people go for care?

My heart was sickened by the suffering of these precious children and their young mothers whose dark, grief-stricken eyes haunted me long after we left the hospital grounds.

Team Ministry at Government Schools

Other days we visited some of the schools where we held chapel services. All the students at each campus crowded into a small classroom with us, where we sang a few worship songs and shared skits. Several from the team shared testimonies about God's love and how He'd helped them, then Pastor Randy Freeman from the Texas team gave a short Scriptural message.

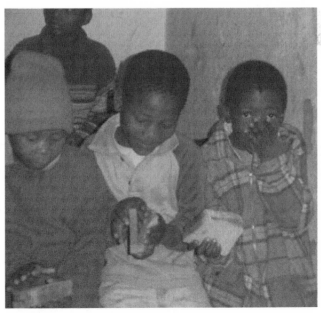

We handed out peanut butter and honey sandwiches on thick brown bread, apples, and bags of potato chips for lunch. We discovered that the lunch was a real treat for the children, who were almost always hungry. During the short break after they ate, we were able to interact individually with the children, some by playing soccer, the favored sport in Swaziland, and others just visiting.

Pastor Stan had encouraged us before we arrived to try to get the children to tell us what they wanted to be when they grew up. My heart broke again when I found that many didn't make any plans for what they'd be when they were older. At that time, only one in every ten children was expected to live to be thirty-six years old. Death was far more familiar to them than anyone attending college or starting a career. But as we probed, some began to toy with the dream of maybe, someday, becoming a pilot, a doctor, a police officer, or a soldier.

One high school girl's laugh still echoes in my mind. She mocked the entire process, arguing with the other children and dashing their hopes for a better future. She then tossed her head, with her short-cropped hair, and announced that she would become a police officer. She seemed to defy anyone to argue with her or say she couldn't do that.

Then she started strutting around, swaying her hips and bragging that she would marry a preacher. She made the other children laugh, because she was obviously the class naughty girl and the least likely to end up with a man of God.

But I quietly approached her and stood face to face, staring into her defiant eyes. I gently cupped her face in my hands and told her that it wouldn't surprise me at all to return to Swaziland one day and find that she was the sweetest, most changed Christian of anyone in the school yard. And yes, even married to a godly pastor she could serve the Lord with while they raised their babies to know Him.

As I shared God's love with her, tears pooled in her eyes. She softened and ended up hugging me tightly as she brushed her tears away. She, like so many others across this tiny nation, needed to hear a few encouraging words from someone who could envision a different outcome for her life. I found myself longing to pour that kind of hope into other Swazi children.

Taking Encouragement to Homes

The chance came to visit some of their homesteads, which was the most astounding education of all.

We approached each homestead with singing, someone in our group carrying loaves of bread to share, and everyone ready to greet the head of the household, which was usually a grandmother, or *gogo*, as they're called in siSwati.

Invariably, they were overcome with joy at our visit, bobbing at the knees in a curtsy as they thanked us repeatedly for coming and graciously received the food we offered.

Most houses were built out of mud and sticks.

Some had a crop of maize growing in a plot near the house, which is the main food staple in Swaziland. It was hard like the field corn we use to feed our cattle here in the States. The Swazis ground the maize/corn to make a porridge very similar in texture to our cream of wheat. A few gardens were also dotted with round green cabbages.

Often there were multiple children dressed in torn clothing, little ones usually bare-bottomed, their noses running over dried snot, their bellies extended. The *gogos* asked them to drag out reed mats for us to sit on outside in the dirt.

We would not have fit inside the tiny two-room huts.

When we asked how we could pray for their families, invariably the women expressed their concerns over being able to feed and educate the children. In most cases, these *gogos* felt like life had played a dirty trick on them. In their culture, their children should have been taking care of them in their old age. Instead, their children had died or deserted the family, leaving the grandmothers who had no income to raise the kids.

We prayed. We wept. And we considered what we could do to make lasting change.

We can't make the facts go away. They are written hard and fast in the history of this kingdom.

But how those statistics play out in the lives of individual people can and must be changed. In spite of efforts to educate Swazis about what causes HIV/AIDS and how to prevent it, many still believe that it's a curse from the ancestors.

They also believe that if an infected person has sex with a virgin, the disease will be cured. Of course, we've never heard of the perpetrators asking about a child's virginity; instead, the perps take what they want and spread the disease.

This leaves children extremely vulnerable. And once they've been raped, the little girls live with such shame, eventually they give in to offers of favors in exchange for sex. Even

33

elementary-aged girls and boys trade their bodies for a meal or one ride to school on the vans that make up the public transport system. Their outlook becomes jaded. Why not ease today's pain a little bit since they don't value their own bodies anymore?

Nobody is watching out for them to make sure they aren't taken advantage of that way. AIDS deaths have produced over 47,000 orphans in Swaziland. But that doesn't even account for the thousands upon thousands of children who are also vulnerable, even though they aren't yet orphaned. Some are caring for sick parents. Others are sick themselves. Many are malnourished. About 45% of the children in Swaziland are deemed to be orphaned or vulnerable children (OVCs).

Many live with relatives who don't want them—sometimes because these adults are sick themselves and/or unable to provide for their own children.

Other kids end up taking care of themselves and younger siblings alone. In 2006, 11% of the homesteads were orphan-led; by 2010, 20% were orphan-led.

To put that in perspective, imagine a small Midwest town with only 1,000 homes in it. What if 200 of those homes had no adult living in them? Who would feed these kids? Where would the food come from? Who would make sure they went to school or did their homework? Who would help them bathe, do the laundry, purchase shoes?

Would anybody sing them a lullaby at bedtime? Read them a story? Tuck them in? Teach them to pray?

Imagine the illness, the grief, the crime that would be bred in such a society.

Then think about what it would look like if half of the other homes in that town were filled with sick people, unable to provide for themselves. Being cared for by more children who didn't know where to find food for the family. Imagine what it would look like if the citizens of the town who actually had jobs made an average of only about $1 per day.

Add to this substandard education standards, superstitious belief systems, and virtually no welfare programs. Then throw in the ever-increasing human trafficking.

That's a picture of Swaziland.

And this is why God "pulled" us to visit this beautiful land.

A casual visit to the hospital, holding chapel at a handful of schools, and making one trip to various homesteads . . . none of that was going to bring lasting change. Deeper relationships grew from the time we spent at Pastor Luendo's church. Our team attended services and hosted a children's rally there. Over 300 kids from all over the mountainside packed out the sanctuary.

Worship in this stucco-like building was inspiring. The praise team was made up of young Swazi adults. The music was loud—the speakers buzzed and thumped with every drumbeat. I honestly wondered if a speaker would blow out during the service. The keyboard was maxed out and played enthusiastically. I got the impression that louder was considered holier.

But the passion of the vocalists as they lifted their songs to heaven was undeniable. I loved the way the leader sang a phrase that was echoed by the rest of the singers and the congregation—a calling back and forth, a give and take of their adoration for the Lord Jesus.

It didn't even matter that I couldn't understand the words to the songs sung in siSwati. Nor did it matter that I often didn't recognize songs sung in English until near the ends of the songs—the accents threw me off at first. I just sang as loudly as I could with whatever words of honor and glory that came to my lips, caught up in the joy of pure praise.

Children shot to their bare feet and danced with zero inhibition, obviously using their entire bodies to show how much they adored the King of kings. The Scripture commanding us to love God with all our hearts, all our souls, and all our strength took on new meaning for me as I observed these little ones giving everything, holding back nothing.

And I had a new awareness of the greatness of our God—so big, worshipped all over the entire earth! I saw that He was not limited by any people group or location. And I basked in the sweetness of His presence.

When the Texas team returned to the States, Tracy, Anna, and I spent most of our time at this site.

And as we connected with people at the church and on that mountain, we found hundreds more wounded souls in the children and adults alike.

Look, I know that we all feel bad when we hear statistics like those you've just read. But every number represents a real child.

Children I've held.

Children I've loved.

Children who still need loving care.

Here are more of their stories.

A Third World
House of Hope

July 2006

Another sea of faces
in a third world house of hope,
Lost in my embraces,
clinging children try to cope.
Bloated bellies, tattered clothes—
their tragic tales unfold.
Fearful eyes reveal the stories
words have never told.

Excerpt from "If You Could See Them Like I See Them"

Seventeen Swazi boys stole my heart.

They lived on Pastor Luendo's homestead, a short walk from the church where we'd enjoyed such beautiful fellowship. You've already heard two of the boys' stories—from Jabu and Colani. This was the care home where they'd both ended up.

Since we were in Swaziland on July 4th, Stan and Sue helped us host a wiener roast to allow the guys to see how we celebrated our independence as a nation back home. We found a store that sold hot dogs. Anna and I were especially excited when we found marshmallows to roast, too.

We made our way up the mountain to set up for the party. Our Toyota Taz bumped along the narrow dirt roads, dodging jagged rocks and gaping holes where the rain had washed them out. Branches screeched as they scraped the sides of our little car. Now and then Tracy had to back up and floor it so he had enough power to ascend the steep places.

Sometimes the cultural differences are huge, and our party was an example of that. Trying to make a special evening for the guys, I had drawn from my childhood experiences when October hayrides and wiener roasts were what memories were made of. At home, preparing a meal over a fire outside was a novelty.

But in Swaziland, it was a normal, everyday occurrence. Thankfully, the evening was still special to the guys, not because of the campfire setting, but because they experienced being celebrated.

They weren't used to that. In fact, many of the guys—and other Swazi children—didn't even know their correct birth dates. They'd never received gifts or decorated cakes or balloons. Nobody had led guests in the birthday song.

Middle child, Titus; child on right, Jabu

So our wiener roast was a special night, not only because of the food we served in ample portions, but also because of the atmosphere. I wasn't naïve enough to assume that one party would be life-changing for the boys. But I did want to communicate that they were valuable enough for the effort and expense.

And oh, boy, was the food ever a hit! Stan grew concerned by the time some of the guys were inhaling their fourth hot dog. He warned them they might want to slow down—or suffer the gastric distress that would surely follow!

At the time, I just thought they were eating a lot because they liked the taste of something different. The hot dogs were nice, but none of them had ever tasted marshmallows before, either. They didn't just eat until they could hold no more; they ate until the food was gone. We certainly didn't have to worry about what to do with leftovers. I didn't realize that they were actually extremely hungry, even though they were in a church care home.

I missed that red flag.

But we were having fun. And I loved watching the boys interact with each other. They had become brothers, bonding through shared suffering. Laughter and teasing, even playful pushing, as boys are apt to do, marked our cookout, all very upbeat. Some of them spoke English well enough that we were able to visit with them. The more fluent interpreted for those who still struggled with our language.

While Sue cleaned up from our meal, I played my guitar and led a few choruses. Then the atmosphere became somber, as one by one, the guys shared their stories.

Colani

Eighteen-year-old Colani was the first one to stand and tell us how he'd ended up at the care center. He picked up a long stick, which he used to stir the coals of the fire. He seemed to need to hold onto something as he spoke. The flames reflected in his dark eyes, and he stood a little straighter when he finally opened his mouth to begin.

He was obviously one of the older boys, taller than the rest and more self-assured. By this time, he had lived at the care home for five years. During the festivities he'd been animated, the life of the party, laughing and teasing the other guys in jest.

We discovered that Colani had quickly shown a talent for interpreting English to SiSwati when he moved to the church. But telling his own story was different.

Now his voice grew softer, raspy as he told us part of the story you read earlier about his terrifying years living in the streets. He relayed the hunger and being chased by street vendors and police officers for stealing.

Even with what he shared, much remained unspoken around the campfire.

He didn't go into detail about the five boys who'd become his brothers. Nor the fears they'd faced daily about being molested by evil men.

He didn't explain how he'd gotten the deep scar across his cheek.

He didn't talk about his feelings of rejection because he had relatives who didn't want him.

He grew quiet, stirring the coals again as he hesitated.

But he took a deep breath and finished the part of his story he could bear to tell, as if he was steeling himself under the heavy burden of grief that had defined his life up to that point.

And as the leader of the group, he had paved the way for the other boys to share their stories, too.

Thando and Ndumiso, Brothers

As soon as eleven-year-old Thando opened his mouth, it was easy to see why his friends at school had nicknamed him "pastor." His short, wiry frame and small features didn't take anything away from his huge personality and gift for gab. Even though he had an infectious smile and loved making everyone laugh, he'd also gained a reputation for preaching to his friends. On the surface, no one would have

guessed the hardships he and his brother Ndumiso had suffered as children.

His first words around the campfire were also lighthearted, and all of us responded to his silliness with chuckles. But when he was ready to share his past, he swallowed hard and cleared his throat a couple of times to choke out his story. He shook his head and gazed into the flames as he took us back in time to his childhood.

Our parents both died when we were very young. Our uncle grudgingly took us into his care, but in a very short time, his wife began beating us over every little offense. She resented having to take responsibility for our care. We didn't gather enough wood for the fire. We took too long hauling the water.

We were too loud. Or we didn't speak up enough. We could never please her.

We didn't get enough food to eat, so we were always still hungry. Our uncle didn't send us to school.

Once he started talking about his mistreatment, Thando's tone reflected the stony resistance he'd developed in response to the abuse. He wasn't shy about uncovering the scars across his back. He lifted his shirt and turned around to reveal the thick marks covering his torso. He stood up even taller, as if daring us to deny his suffering. He assured us that Ndumiso had wounds to match.

When I was seven years old, Ndumiso and I finally felt ready to run away from the homestead, so we took our opportunity to escape. We hid in the forest near the village, foraging for berries and other edible foods we could find.

Eventually our situation was reported to the police, who picked us up. They looked for a safer place for Ndumiso and me to live. We ended up in Pastor Luendo's care.

Even though Ndumiso is three years older than Thando, his narrative about what they'd experienced was told so quietly, I couldn't hear much of anything he said. He kept his eyes down most of the time, only glancing up furtively now and then to make very brief eye contact with me, quickly retreating back into his protective walls.

At first I thought he was afraid or possibly ashamed. But during his brief speech, I realized from his slumped shoulders and timidity that the essence of his demeanor was actually woundedness. Watching Ndumiso was worse than seeing a dog that has been beaten so that it shrinks back in fear when someone lifts a hand. I was watching someone who had been beaten past the point of fear, past a broken will, all the way to a completely broken spirit.

While Thando's response to the abuse was, "You can't break me," Ndumiso's response was to shut down. He wasn't only beaten physically; he was beaten down emotionally, succumbing to feelings of worthlessness and rejection.

And why wouldn't he feel that way? His parents were gone, leaving him to fend for himself, unable to protect his little brother. Relatives who should've cared for his grieving soul instead lashed out at him, as though he'd done something wrong just because he needed them. Nothing could hide the hopelessness in his dark brown eyes. He'd given up.

And every maternal instinct in me rose up with the desire to show him that he was valuable, wanted, worth anything I could do or give him.

Worth the life and blood and death of the very Son of God.

People had done this to Ndumiso. God would use people to restore him.

But it wouldn't happen easily—or quickly.

Menzie

Menzie was fifteen when we met him during this first visit to Swaziland. Almost every picture we took of him showed his arms crossed tightly across his chest. But he didn't come across as a defiant teenager; he seemed more like a little boy trying to protect himself. And when we learned his story, pieced together from several conversations with him, we understood why.

I lived with both of my parents in Mbabane, the capital of Swaziland. Our mud and stick house was on the outskirts of the city in a sort of shanty town.

Their marriage was unstable from the start. In Swaziland, a man is supposed to pay his bride's family a dowry in cows— usually fifteen of them.

Those who follow the old ways take this very seriously; the wife's family can even take the children if the dowry is unpaid, even though so few men can afford to follow the custom.

My father never paid even one cow, and there were ill feelings toward him from my mother's family. I grew up always embarrassed of the omission. I determined from a young age that I would never treat my future wife and her family with such disrespect.

My parents ended up divorcing, and my mother became engaged to another man. I lived with them, but I always feared that my grandparents would come to take me away since the dowry had never been paid.

Both of my parents died, with the dowry issue unresolved. I continued to live with my stepfather. I had nowhere else to go. I began to realize that I had never been in any danger of being taken from my mother. My grandparents didn't want me.

Life on that homestead was not easy. My stepfather was very abusive to me. He shouted at me. He beat me for every little thing. He even chased me off the homestead sometimes.

I finally ran away to stay on the streets in Mbabane. I think I was seven or eight years old when I left.

I never slept in the same place two nights in a row. Mostly I stayed beside stores downtown. I had to steal food and beg to stay alive. I was cold or hot, depending on the weather. During the rainy season, I was so wet and cold, I thought I would die. I didn't have a blanket or any warm clothes.

Every now and then some kind person would pay attention to me. But even when I was holding out my hands and begging for a bite to eat, most people walked on by. Too many of us kids were asking for help.

Later, my uncle took me to live with him for a while in Malkerns. It was a long distance from Mbabane. I could tell that he cared about me, but he didn't have enough money to take care of me. We stayed in a one-room house with his girlfriend. Sometimes they made me sleep outside.

Finally, because I was still hungry and often in the elements, I ran away again to live on the streets.

I kept myself alive, but I was miserable and alone. After about three or four years mostly on the streets, when I was eleven years old, a white man found me in the streets and took me to Challenge Ministries. I was referred to Pastor Luendo's church by Pastor Kevin's staff, because I was too young to stay with the older men.

When life tells you that you're not worth the time and effort to have your most basic needs met, the enemy of your soul is quick to pounce on that lie with whispers and accusations to confirm it. Menzie tried to fill the hole of rejection in his heart with someone who would show him love and affection. By the time we met him, he had already been in trouble because of his behavior with girls.

It was a poor counterfeit for the Love waiting to heal him from the inside out.

Musa

Fending for yourself as a child is one type of hardship.

Caring for children when you're still a child yourself is another. And it's just as real. I know. Because I was that kind of child.

My mother only had one child: me.

But I had other brothers and sisters, because my father had other wives.

When he took a new one, my mother abandoned me, leaving my father to raise me while she married someone else.

When my father died, nine of us children were left behind. None of our mothers remained to care for us.

We lived in the mud and stick house with a thatch roof that our father had built. All nine of us were cramped together to live and eat and sleep in one small space.

We depended on handouts from neighbors, but most people in our area of the mountain were also in need.

I had one sister who was older than me, named Nomtandazo. She dropped out of high school after completing only form 1 so she could take care of the younger children. That left her with four forms unfinished, so she couldn't find a job for a very long time.

As the next oldest, I became the man of the house, doing as much as I could to help provide food for the seven younger children.

Every morning, I arose early to hurry down the mountain at a full run. It took me forty-five minutes to get to my primary school, and I was drenched in sweat, even in cold weather. I paid attention in class the best I could, although I was often drowsy.

After the last class of the day, I ran another thirty minutes, also at full speed, to get to the business where I served as a night security guard. When my shift was over in the middle of the night, I still had to run back home to try to sleep for a little while before the whole routine started over again when the sun came up.

Eventually Nomtandazo was able to find a job cleaning the courthouse six days a week. Her pay was equivalent to about $65 per month. It wasn't much for so many children, but it helped us keep going. Like me, she also had to travel on foot a great distance to her job, making her leave the children early in the mornings and arrive back at home very late at night, many times after the little ones had already drifted off to sleep.

Everyone had to help care for the smaller children. We cooked our maize inside over a fire, and the walls of our hut were blackened. All of us took turns gathering firewood, carrying water, washing clothes by hand, and hanging them over bushes to dry.

The very young kids left at home during the day were vulnerable to older children and adults on the mountain making unsolicited visits.

When I was at school, my mind wandered. Even at night when I was at work, watching for possible intruders at the business, my thoughts would turn to home. I was always worried about what was happening back there while my sister and I were gone. We had no security guards watching out for intruders on our homestead.

As the children grew taller, we knew we had to have more space to live in. Over time, I was finally able to patch together two more simple mud and stick structures to give more space to our family.

When I was eighteen years old, David Wilkinson launched a gardening project in Swaziland. Some of his team helped plant gardens in our village. I eagerly helped the American men who came; I carried supplies for them and pitched in with soil preparation and planting. One of the men volunteering, Bobby, seemed to like me and said he was impressed with me.

He knew how difficult it was for older children like me to get help; most people are moved by the faces of the younger children who seem so lost. But older kids are just as needy. Without an education, we are trapped in poverty. So, when it was time for him to return to the US, Bobby started crying. He was worried about what would happen to me. He asked

Pastor Luendo to let me live at the church care home, even though I was older than the other guys.

Pastor Luendo agreed. My move improved my chances for an education. But it created a hardship for Nomtandazo, who was still trying to feed the other seven siblings. I tried to visit the homestead as often as possible on the weekends so I could at least lend a hand.

I was torn between the obvious immediate needs of the children, and the long-term doors that could open for me if I passed all the way through form 5 in high school. I knew that if I did, I might be able to study in a university to give me a better option for employment. Then I could provide the important educational expenses to help the children later.

Musa gave up his childhood so his brothers and sisters would live to have one. As his story unfolded, I couldn't help comparing his life with my own teenaged sons. Teenagers are still growing and need to sleep. How was Musa managing to stay awake in class? When did he study? How could he pass? My heart went out to him, a young man barely past adolescence, laying down his life so his younger brothers and sisters wouldn't starve to death. He already had my loyalty.

Sibusiso

Unknown.

If one word could describe how I felt as a child, this would be the one.

Not that I didn't try to seem happy around other people, especially when I got older. I smiled almost nonstop, even with strangers.

But my life was a big question mark.

I never knew my father. I was told that he passed away when I was very young.

I never knew any of my father's relatives, either. I have always felt a big hole in my life from that.

I remember only a little bit about my mother, because she didn't live with me. My uncle took care of me while my mother worked in another town. She tried to visit me as much as she could. I always stayed by her side instead of playing with my friends. I missed her too much to leave her. When she would return to her job, I would cry a long time.

When I was only six years old, she also died. I can't even remember what she looked like.

My grandmother tried to care for me, but she was also very ill, so we moved in with my uncle.

This was a difficult time, because they didn't have enough food for all of us. I did piece jobs for different people to earn a little bit of money for food, fetching firewood and water, but we were always hungry.

I tried to keep going to school, but I was too hungry to learn. I sometimes hid in the bushes alone instead of going to class. I was growing bitter and felt sure there was no God.

My best friend Bongane sometimes skipped school with me so we could go to his house. His mother had a job, so they had food to eat. He knew I was always hungry, so he cooked for me. He almost always had bread and juice to share with me. I wish I could see him again sometime to apologize for not saying goodbye when I left that area, and also to thank him for his kindness.

When I was seven years old, my granny also died. Often my uncle would tell me there wasn't going to be any food all day. I finally had to quit going to school at all.

I dreamed that a man would show up at the house and say, "I'm your father." I just couldn't accept that I would never know him. And I needed someone to step in to take care of me.

In a short time, my uncle said I couldn't live with him much longer. He had too many children to feed, so I was a burden. I was afraid. What would happen to me? Where would I go?

I thought maybe if I worked harder for food, maybe I wouldn't have to leave. So I kept asking neighbors to let me do little jobs for them. But they took advantage of my young age and situation, often giving me only half a piece of bread just to keep me barely alive.

Many people thought I would die, and I agreed with them. In fact, I decided I must have been born to die young.

Watching my friends with families was painful, especially at Christmas. They received new clothes, but I was still wearing the same clothes my mother and grandmother had given me. They were rags that didn't fit anymore, and I was ashamed. I hid most of Christmas Day.

I found three new friends who had money from their parents. They purchased benzin, a liquid made from petroleum. We got high on it, and I felt like I had no problems anymore. Soon the boys started buying daggai [marijuana]. I smoked it with them for about eight months, but when the boys quit giving it to me, I had no money to buy more, so I quit.

When I looked at my reflection, I wondered who I was. Did my big brown eyes resemble someone in my family? Did I have my father's ears? My mother's nose? My grandpa's laugh? Did I jut out my hand exactly the way my aunt did when I told a story?

Finally, a friend of my mother's, Make [Mrs./Mama] Sibisi, said she would take me. But I didn't live with her; she had a young son living on the mangwaneni [squatter's camp] on the outskirts of Mbabane. I moved in with him. I was older than Thembu and became his caregiver. Make and Babe [Mr./Papa] Sibisi lived with their daughter in another town where they had jobs. They visited us at the end of every month.

But food was still an issue. Thembo went to school, but I didn't get to go. I found jobs. Early in the morning I would help a sick girl by escorting her to school, carrying her bag. This provided the boy and me with some food, but not enough.

So I began walking into town to steal from shop owners. One day I was caught at the Spar [a grocery store at the mall]. As I walked out of the store, I was stopped for a search. When security found food hidden in my pockets, they asked why I was stealing. I told them I was poor, and at the moment, I was hungry. They beat me badly and told me to get away.

While the boy was at school, I was lonely. I had no friends. When some of my peers wanted to play, I beat them up. I was bitter and hurting so much inside, all I wanted to do was hurt someone else. I hated being called an orphan. People taunted me because my mother died with HIV. I felt rejected and broken inside.

Sometimes the Sibisi boy shared his clothes with me. He appreciated me, because I protected him when someone wanted to beat him. We bonded like brothers, and I loved him.

I started attending a church in the area where we lived. The pastor there worked for Challenge Ministries. When he learned I wasn't in school, he wanted to hear my story. He encouraged me not to give up.

He ended up talking to Make and Babe Sibisi, who cared about what happened to me. I heard that at some point they also talked to my aunt, but she didn't want to provide for me. And my uncle who had let me stay with him for a while had died.

So the pastor advised Babe Sibisi to talk to someone at Challenge Ministries. Babe learned that they had no space for me, but they promised to look for someone to help.

One day as I sat thinking about my life, crying and wondering why I was created, I heard a knock on the door. A man stood there and told me to pack my bags; I was going to a new home.

The pastor of the church also came, and he told me to take care of myself. I started crying harder. I had already been taking care of myself! But at least I had someone to love, and the boy loved me back! Now I was going to a strange place, and I wondered if it would be worse than where I was. I had been passed around for four years, but that was familiar to me.

As we headed up a mountain to the village where I would stay, my fears grew. Bumping along, I tried to remember what direction we had come from in case I needed to get away.

We arrived during a church service where Pastor Luendo was preaching. After the service, I was immediately given clothes that fit me and was assigned a bed. There were other boys like me living there, boys who had also been through hardships and understood me.

We became as close as brothers, and my bitterness gradually vanished, replaced with peace and happiness because I was loved by them. One boy, Menzie, became very close to me.

I was finally able to go to school. I didn't have to take care of anyone else.

I still ached to know something about my father, and I hoped to meet some of his relatives someday. The big question mark about him had left me wondering who I was for ten years.

But I started believing that God had a plan even for me. My background didn't matter. I was the same in His eyes as everyone else.

And finally, I hoped I might stay in one place long enough to fit in.

Maybe I would even be wanted.

Sibusiso's life wasn't like that of a child who is adopted. In adoption, the child has the chance to begin to pick up the mannerisms and speech patterns of the new family. Not that there aren't issues, because there are. But that situation has potential for a sense of belonging, and hopefully, even some answers about the birth family when the child is old enough to wonder.

Sibusiso had been passed around too much to develop those kinds of roots. He ached to know.

Like many children longing for attachment, Sibusiso was easy to be around. Pleasant.

But I noticed that he frequently thanked us for every little thing we did. Not that I dislike gratitude—it's an important character trait! And he was sincere. But again, I compared his reactions to my children at home. Of course, I was always glad when at least one of my eight children thanked me for supper, which usually followed with the others chiming in, "Yeah, thanks, Mom." But that would be the end of it.

Sibusiso, in contrast, would go on and on, thanking us profusely for a meal, "Eesh, no, I can't even find the words to tell you thank you enough. Really, what you have done has touched me so deeply. You have given me a treasure." And so on.

I suspected that he felt obligated to respond to every "scrap" of attention, careful to express how glad he was to have it, instead of realizing that when you're loved, having your needs met is part of the package.

I hoped God's plans for us would give me the opportunity to show him enough loving care that he would begin to understand that simple truth based on God's incredible love within us.

And hopefully, that would lead to this sweet young man finding his identity, after all. Known.

And loved just like he is.

A Better Place to Live

The stories of the ten other guys living at the church care home also gripped us as we saw the same patterns of abandonment, abuse, and neglect repeated in their lives. Tracy and I found ourselves heartbroken. We prayed fervently, asking God how we could help Pastor Luendo make a lasting difference in their lives. He was willing to take even more young men, but finding the finances to send them to school and feed them was challenging.

All seventeen of the guys stayed in a long, wooden shack beside the pastor's house, but it was so dilapidated, Pastor Luendo wouldn't even allow us to peek in. New structures had been started for them just behind the church; however, like many projects in Swaziland, they hadn't been finished. These new homes were small huts that could hold four boys each when completed.

Tracy and I were very interested in what it would take to finish the huts for the guys.

Since we were staying for a whole month, we thought maybe we could make some progress after the rest of our team departed.

Because our team was so large, I hadn't noticed that the guys didn't eat with us in the house. They hung around though, happy to show us the chickens and rabbits they took care of and eager to answer our questions. Most of them were all smiles, eating up the attention. I looked forward to getting to know them for the duration of our stay.

And we got to do exactly that. In fact, we spent most of the rest of our time at this church site, filling holes in the plaster of the huts, painting, and moving the project forward.

I was feeling pretty safe and relieved that we weren't using a machete to cut our way through the forest to reach anyone, as I'd imagined any stint in Africa would entail. Nevertheless, while we worked on the huts in this relatively developed area, I happened upon one of those horrifying spiders the size of a man's hand! The creepy thing was clinging to the outside wall of one of the huts, about eye level with me. I can still feel my goosebumps and the scream that traveled up my throat—as well as the sound of Tracy crunching the arachnid with a two-by-four! (If you're thinking about going with us to Swaziland, trust me when I tell you, I've never seen another one in the fifteen trips I've taken. Don't let fear keep you away!)

Stopping to kill the spider wasn't the only deterrent to our progress. Tracy is a bit of a perfectionist. He's a machinist, so he's used to measuring to the thousandth of an inch. Suffice it to say that building in Swaziland is not precise. We used multiple buckets of spackling to fill in gaps.

Part of being a perfectionist is taking plenty of time to get a job done right. Yes, that's my nice way of saying that Tracy works slowly. Ha-ha! But slow took on an entirely new meaning for us during our stint on this project.

We got up early every day so we could pick up supplies as soon as the hardware store opened. We perused the dusty shelves and checked out what was stacked in heaps on the floor. Unlike stores back at home, no employees stopped by to ask if they could help. When we sought one out, we discovered that we had to get past the language barriers. Even though they spoke English, some items went by different names in Swaziland. And when we asked employees to come to see what we were talking about, their slow gait nearly drove us nuts. We experienced firsthand a quote I've come to appreciate: "Nothing happens fast in Africa." We waited for help with our selections, waited in line to pay, and waited for the loading our purchases.

We would finally get to the site about 9 or 9:30 am, with Tracy eager to get started. Since it was their winter, and this was on a mountain, he knew it would start getting dark by around 4:30 pm. Daylight was burning!

But upon our arrival, invariably Pastor Luendo and his wife would greet us with an invitation to come inside for tea. This would turn into an hour of visiting, getting to know each other, and fellowship. We experienced for the first time the crunchy cookies Swazis called biscuits, thanks to the British influence in southern Africa. We also drank the strong rooibos tea with milk in it—also an English practice. Tracy tried hard not to look at his watch between bites and gulps, but he was challenged to sit still and visit.

It was just one more glimpse of how different our cultures are. Americans and many westerners tend to be project-oriented. We see what needs done, and we set out to accomplish it. We estimate how long the project will take and compare that with how many days we have available to work, eager to plan our time around the end goal.

Swazis and many developing countries, however, tend to put relationships before projects. To them, spending that hour sharing our lives was time very well spent.

It didn't make one of us right and the other wrong; it just showed how differently we thought. We learned from each other. We were stretched.

Thankfully, even with the delays, we were able to get the project far enough along that just a couple of months after our return home, the huts were completed by our missionary friend Stan Drew and some Swazi workers. The boys were finally able to move in.

Ministry Direction

During this first trip, I had an open heart and mind to the people. I didn't want to arrogantly assume that our ways in the US were superior to what I saw in Swaziland. So even when something bothered me, I attributed my uneasiness to cultural differences. I wanted to learn and serve and love.

After all, I wasn't there to pass judgment of any kind. I was there to find out why God had sent us on this trip and what He wanted us to do when the month was over.

Besides, I could see how much better off these young men were because they were living at the church care center. They'd all been rescued from unthinkable situations. And they were in an environment where they would hear the Good News of Jesus regularly. I could see that they had become a brotherhood, forged through similar past hardships.

At the end of our month in Swaziland, we still didn't know for sure everything the Lord intended for us to do, but we knew we couldn't go home and forget the beautiful faces of the Swazi children. We had to help where we could, and it seemed clear that we could start with a sponsorship program. This would at least pay for school fees, supplies, uniforms, and shoes so they could attend school, where hopefully they would also receive one meal every day.

Through the years, we'd sponsored children through Compassion International, so we were familiar with that kind of program. Honestly, we wondered why He would want to use us—just plain old Tracy and Becky Spencer from little Buhler, Kansas. The answer? Because Compassion and other organizations hadn't helped these particular children yet, and they couldn't wait. He was willing to use us, because we were willing to let Him.

We were glaringly aware that we couldn't do it alone. So, we founded Grand Staff Ministries to give us a vehicle through which to serve the children.

We had a vision of the orphaned, abandoned, and vulnerable children in Swaziland, so much like little lost lambs. And we knew that the Good Shepherd's staff was grand enough—great enough—to meet every need.

But His plan was to do it through people.

Through me, and through you.

Expanding Our Service

2008 - 2013

The needs are overwhelming,
My meager gifts too few,
My grandeur plans defective;
There is far too much to do.
My heart sinks, 'cause I know
My work will barely make a dent.

Excerpt from "If You Could See Them Like I See Them"

During the first few months after returning home, some of our family members and close friends joined us to sponsor all seventeen boys at Pastor Luendo's site. For two years we stayed in touch with him via email and an occasional phone call. In 2008 we returned to Swaziland. We were eager to see "our boys" again.

Reconnecting with them was a primary focus of this journey, but we were also ready to take pictures of new children and put together short histories for each one. We would add children from the church where our guys lived, then branch out to other churches recommended by Stan and Sue. With the masses of children in need, we simply had to reach more of them.

We were stepping into new territory. Taking care of our seventeen guys was relatively easy. But so many children were waiting . . . I didn't want them to become "another sea of faces." I wanted to know each one, to love them as individuals, to bring Jesus to them in practical ways they could comprehend.

I have to admit that I learned my limitations quickly. Every time we were in public, whether we were buying groceries, eating at a restaurant, attending church, or even just parking our car, we were approached by desperate people begging us to help them. I didn't want to become jaded, nor did I want to fall for scams. But the sheer numbers, compared with the resources we had to work with, exhausted me.

Some days I felt like a sow, with a huge litter of piglets scrambling all over me, oinking and fighting for a place to latch on for sustenance.

I needed to learn how to love the children by God's grace, not in my own strength.

I think I was in His remedial class.

But He is a patient and thorough Teacher. He was showing me how to see the children the way He sees them.

> If you could see them like I see them,
> You'd see all I dreamed they would be.
> You'd see the gifts I placed inside,
> You'd understand My sense of pride,
> And all the joy they give to Me.
>
> If you could see them like I see them,
> You'd love one of them in My Name.
> You'd give your life just to free them,
> Imagine how it feels to be them,
> If you could see them like I see them.

Excerpt from "If You Could See Them Like I See Them"

He wanted me to see each child like I see my own children and grandchildren. That would give me the grace I needed to lay down my life for them, one at a time.

Making it personal would also help define the way we interacted with the new children being added to the program. We would spend time with each one like we had with our boys, asking questions, listening to them, holding the little ones, hugging everyone, making eye contact.

Pastor Luendo wasn't the only clergyman to have children dropped off at his church door. It was common in Swaziland because of the AIDS crisis, especially after a pastor agreed to take the first one.

Their standing in their communities also put these men in a position to hear stories of real needs from the relatives who were willing to take the kids, even though they couldn't afford to provide the basics for the orphaned and vulnerable children living with them. Food was already scarce in most homesteads.

And like in most other African countries, schooling was not free. Eventually the government claimed to provide a free education to elementary students, but the schools managed to come up with reasons to charge them building fees, top-off funds, and so on. High school students had to pay rising costs of tuition, lab fees, book rentals, and class trips. Plus every student had to wear the required uniforms and shoes.

People turned to the pastors, hoping, somehow, they could help give the children an opportunity for a better future.

So, taking Stan's advice, we chose to expand our sponsorship program based in churches. For one thing, it seemed the pastors would be the most trustworthy source for information and administration of the program. It was also our best hope to include a godly element to the upbringing of every child.

We didn't want to merely educate kids; we wanted to disciple godly leaders who would impact the Swazi culture with the love of God and His truth that brings deliverance.

Deep down, we sensed that every child needed four strong elements in his or her life in order to succeed: home, church, school, and the funding Grand Staff Ministries (GSM) could bring to facilitate the rest. Not one of the four could provide what the other three needed to supply. But if done well by all, the child would find the kind of stability needed to build a better future.

With those four elements in mind, we came up with guidelines for our sponsorship program. Children were required to attend church. If they failed a grade twice, we would need to remove them from sponsorship. We would hire Swazi ministry partners to visit the homesteads to ensure the children were being supervised and cared for. And of course, we would continue to seek additional sponsors.

The expansion of our program took us to four additional Swazi churches in very different environments, each with its own mini-culture.

Manzini

The largest urban center in Swaziland is Manzini, home to about 110,000 people. The first time we made the twenty-five-minute drive south from our cottage, the smells of garbage, waste, and unwashed humanity assaulted our senses about ten kilometers before we reached the city limits. I was thankful to have scented hand sanitizer, not for the antibacterial properties at that moment, but so I could scratch my nose and sniff the black cherry smells to mask the scent of filth.

The modern Riverside Mall, one of the first landmarks seen entering the city, gave the false impression of prosperity. But venturing further into the downtown area showed another story. People crowded the busy streets, ignoring the honking horns and cars bearing down on them as they jaywalked in groups. Parking looked nearly impossible, and hurried drivers didn't seem to mind a dent or two.

Trash littered the sidewalks. Children and drunks begged outside of businesses. Dirty stores featuring blankets, electronics, and cheap shoes competed for business from the pedestrians who had walked a long way to shop.

We continued driving to the other end of the city, turning off on the southeast outskirts of Manzini to enter the *mangwaneni*. It's what we would call a squatter's camp. Several *mangwanenis* exist in Swaziland. The poorest of the poor live in these areas the king has allotted for people who have no homestead.

This one was located directly across the street from the dump. And that's where we were supposed to find The Faithful Church, our next partnership connection.

We had to drive very slowly to maneuver through the chaos, watching for unsupervised children so we wouldn't accidentally run into one.

We'd been told that anyone who could find a little piece of land in this area was allowed to put up a hut or house to live in. Others rented places that had been vacated.

What we saw confirmed the stories we'd heard about life in the *mangwaneni*.

Hopelessness was tangible.

Huts were squeezed closely together. Trash was more common than grass. Broken glass, rusted cans, and garbage were piled in every available space. Even the carcasses of gutted cars crowded some of the yards, evidence of better times now gone.

Most homesteads were headed by *gogos* or single mothers. Unemployment was high, obvious by the men congregated sporadically, finally awake in the afternoon after drinking home-brewed marula beer well into the night. Thankfully, we didn't witness any fights breaking out.

I was out of my comfort zone.

But when we carefully pulled past the metal gate of the church yard, preschool and primary school-aged children swarmed our car, eager to give hugs, hoping for sweets, smiling ear to ear. Clearly, they felt welcomed and safe behind the gate.

That helped us feel safe, as well. Several structures lined the perimeter of the fence defining the church's property. There was no grass, but in the circle of dirt in the middle of the buildings, a large kettle hung over a makeshift fire. Women washed clothes in plastic tubs, using a long green bar of soap to scrub each piece, rinsing them in another tub, and hanging them to dry on a makeshift line.

Pastor Jacinto Sambo ambled over and joined the kids greeting us as we got out of our car. His slow smile and peaceful demeanor settled over my spirit as we warmly grasped hands. We visited for a few minutes, and he shared how he'd moved his wife Angelina and their eight children from Mozambique to Swaziland, answering the call of God to serve the needy families in the *mangwaneni*.

He pointed to the buildings, explaining which ones his family lived in, showing us the tiny one functioning as his office, and making sure we knew that the two doors hanging crookedly from their hinges on a small shack were the boys' and girls' outhouses. As we neared that structure, our noses confirmed the function of the facility. I found myself hoping that Anna and I wouldn't need to visit that building. But then I chided myself; it was so much better than trying to find a place to squat outside in bushes. The church was blessed to have the outhouses.

Pastor Sambo then gave us a tour of the thriving preschool held inside his church. The little ones quickly took their places, and we were delighted when they performed songs for us and quoted Bible verses in English. When we handed out care packages, each child lined up orderly and bobbed in a little curtsy while chiming, "Thank you very much."

Pastor Sambo then explained some of the ways they were trying to reach the families in door-to-door ministry, handing out candles and matches to every home while sharing the message of the Light of the world. He was hopeful that change would come to the *mangwaneni,* one heart at a time.

And he was eager to partner with us so the children would have a chance to improve their lives. He assured us that while the education was important, so was the actual school attendance. Children would be safer in school than they were hanging around the camp where they were vulnerable targets of evil.

So we started the process of meeting the children and getting to know them. And for each child, there was a story.

- An adorable six-year-old girl had living parents, but they were unemployed and raising eight children. Some of the kids on this homestead were nieces and nephews they were responsible for. Others shared the same mother, but different fathers. All were hungry. Could we at least get this little one into school?

- A nine-year-old boy was only in second grade. His father abandoned the family, and his mom was raising three children alone. This little guy struggled in school because he was so hungry. Could we help pay his fees, provide some food, and arrange for a tutor before he got any further behind?

- Several girls were suspected of trading their bodies for food, phones, airtime, rides to town, clothing . . . it wasn't uncommon. Prostitution was rampant in the *mangwaneni*. Most of the girls had already been raped, so in their pain and shame and need, they saw their bodies as bargaining tools. Could we help set them on a new path by providing daily needs?

- The grandmother of orphaned twins died. Could we help purchase large pots, bunk beds, and blankets so the pastor could build a small structure on the site for his oldest daughter to move into with them? And could we get them into school?

- A high school boy's parents died. His aunt didn't want him in her home. So he was forced to live in a two-room house alone. No food, no electricity, no love, no hugs. School was challenging. But he was motivated to learn. Could we supply food and pay his school fees?

- A high school girl was receiving treatments for tuberculosis. She was missing too much class, and she wasn't a very good student, anyway. After she finished her treatment at the hospital, could we help her take a catering course so she could become a server in a restaurant?

- Another high school girl ran away from home with her boyfriend and contracted AIDS. She died. Her father died soon after from diabetes complications. Her mother was trying to gather bottles to clean up and sell, but she wasn't making enough to feed her remaining son. Could we help him get to school?

- Two girls were being forced to attend a church where members were beaten. Could these girls still be in the program, since they had no choice about what church they attended?
- This sweet boy had lots of stepbrothers and sisters, and his parents were separated. He lived with his unemployed father, who appeared to have a serious drinking problem. The boy suffered from frequent headaches and nasal problems. Could we get him to a doctor and somehow keep him in school?
- Oh, this girl, ready to start high school, was very smart! Her mother was a nurse and used to send her to school, even though her dad left them. But her brother had been hit by a car and needed continual care in order to survive his severe injuries. Her mom couldn't work like she used to, and there were five children to care for. Could we help this girl reach her dreams of getting an education so she could become a nurse like her mother? And could we help with the ongoing medical expenses for this injured boy?

More stories, many similar to these, broke our hearts.

We were convinced that the *mangwaneni* was a place of fear, lack, abuse, and darkness.

We wrote out the biographies for each child and took pictures to put in a notebook of children waiting for help. And we prayed that we would be able to find sponsors for all of them when we returned home.

Over time, God answered that prayer. At first, we focused on getting the children into school, which did more than educate them; it also gave them something to do all day so they were less vulnerable to mistreatment.

Sponsorship became a tiny flame in the night.

Bhunya

The town of Bhunya is nestled between small mountains about an hour's drive from the capital. It was best known for the lumber mill, which provided many jobs and boosted the economy. When the mill closed in 2010 due to a poor market

and a forest fire, every business was affected. Of course, when workers were no longer earning, they couldn't afford to shop in the stores anymore.

The city had about 3,000 residents, so when 500 mill workers lost their jobs, that was one-sixth of the population. And the mill owned about 1,000 houses; besides the mill workers, they also employed people to work in the forests before the shutdown.

We made the drive to Walk by Faith Church, enjoying the streams gurgling beside the steep dirt road leading up to the church grounds. Pastor Jan (pronounced John) Dvube welcomed Tracy and me to step under the roofed area where the church held services. One of the first things that struck me was the large percentage of *gogos*, mamas, and aunties who were present for our meeting with the children. Even a few fathers and grandfathers were present, evidence of the commitment these families had to educating their children.

They were seated on simple homemade wooden benches without backs. A few children were shooed away quickly to make space for us to be seated. Handmade cement blocks were stacked in the churchyard, waiting to become the walls that would provide protection from weather and the distraction of cows and goats wandering by.

We learned that the church was started with nightly tent meetings lasting several weeks. The people who received Jesus during those meetings became the core group joining Pastor Jan in the church plant.

They were eager to partner with Grand Staff Ministries, because many of the families in the church had been affected by the closing of the mill. It left them desperate to find a way to pay for school for their active youth and children. Without an education, options for the future would be limited.

As we interviewed the Bhunya children and their caregivers, we found more sad stories.

- A nine-year-old boy had dropped out of school. His parents were never married, and his father was already a married man. This boy lived with his mother and his three half-siblings; two of their fathers were deceased. All of them lived with his grandmother, and no one in the family had a job. Could we help this boy get back into school?
- An eight-year-old girl had never met her father. She and her mother lived with her *gogo*. Her mother loved the Swazi traditional *Umhlanga*, which was the annual, eight-day reed dance. Tens of thousands of unmarried girls, starting at age six, sang and danced bare-breasted and with short skirts showing their bottoms, in front of the king, dignitaries, and tourists. The king could choose a new queen from the dancers if he so desired. This mother dreamed of her daughter becoming the next queen, removing their poverty. Meanwhile, this innocent little girl just

wanted to attend school. Her dream was to become a nurse. Could we provide schooling in case the mom needed a back-up plan to becoming royalty?

- A seventh-grade boy was deserted by his father, and his mother was in a car accident. That left his *gogo* trying to care for six children. He hoped we could help with his schooling so he could possibly have some pocket money from his relatives. They couldn't afford to give him even a little bit of change, since they struggled to pay for his education. I wondered if he would buy candy or cans of pop if he were to have any spending money, so I asked him what he would he do with it. He replied he'd buy ice so the food at home would be safe to eat.

- Two sisters in primary school lost both of their parents to disease. Their auntie was trying to take care of them, but she was also sick. The girls spent lots of time at the church, helping clean and carry firewood. Members of the congregation helped provide some food, but they desperately needed more. Could we pay for their schooling and supplement the food supply?

- One primary student, a boy, passed out at church on a Sunday morning. The women revived him and learned that he hadn't eaten since Friday morning at school. There was no food in the home. They scrounged up something for him to eat that day, but could we help this family with food and schooling for the boy?

We were shown report cards from Bhunya schools and noticed that children who were at the top of their classes were still failing many or even most of their subjects. It turned out that the schools weren't supplying enough textbooks for every student. So besides paying school fees, we obviously also needed to purchase books that could be used and passed down every year to children in the sponsorship program.

We took time to visit some homesteads while we were in Bhunya. We saw evidence of happier times when there was more prosperity. Some residents had nice homes to live in, plastered instead of just mud and sticks. Some had store-bought furniture and maybe even evidence of once having electricity, but their boom boxes sat silently on the shelves.

Sadly, no amount of possessions from days gone by would fill a hungry belly or pay school fees.

Nor could those items remove the disease that kept desperate mothers shivering under blankets in makeshift beds in the living areas of the homes we visited. We saw with our own eyes what was meant when Swaziland was described as being ravaged by AIDS.

So we were ready to be the bridge between the needs of these innocent children and the abundance back at home in the States. Tracy and I reminded ourselves that the Lord wasn't asking us to carry the whole load; He wanted us to see, and then share. Again we prayed that He would lead us to people who would demonstrate compassion by loving a child practically in His Name.

And again, He was faithful. He led us to beautiful people through contacts made in our bed and breakfast, at Christian writers' conferences, and in our church. Uniforms and shoes were purchased, school tuitions were paid, and smiles were abundant on the faces of these children.

They were starting to believe that maybe they could recapture the dreams for the future they used to hold dear.

Mangcongco

In 2013, we added the village of Mangcongco to our sponsorship program. This is a church plant of Bhunya's Walk by Faith Church. Even higher in the mountains, the roads are flanked by forests planted for commerce.

This rural area is much poorer than Bhunya. Very few people have jobs, and most subsist by farming their own crops. The drought in Swaziland has deeply affected these villagers. They have to carry water from streams or rivers, and it's impossible to tote enough for the crops. Most families don't have electricity.

But during our first visit, the people were warm and quickly bonded with us. Most of the children here were being raised by their *gogos* who came to our meeting. These women loved to make jokes with me and laugh together. I enjoyed the camaraderie they shared with one another, and they made a point to include me.

The people were extremely hungry for God's Word. They hadn't had a consistent pastor or preacher, which left them like sheep without a shepherd. During one of our visits, when Tracy and I were the only ones who made the trip, they invited me to share with them on a Sunday morning.

It happened to be very cold that day in the mountains—the coldest day we'd ever experienced in Swaziland. Many of the children were barefoot, as were even some of the adults. Others had only flip-flops. Few had sneakers or anything warm on their feet. And some of the little ones were scantily clad—they don't all have a selection of clothes.

Still, these precious people insisted that we let them wrap a blanket around our laps and feet. We tried to get them to use it themselves, but they refused. They so appreciated our coming, they wanted to honor us. Such hospitality!

About eighty people crowded into a round hut. At least being so close helped them warm up a bit. But even the children hung on every word of Scripture, devouring the truth they so desperately longed for.

We were humbled by their burning desire to hear God's Word. How many westerners have Bibles on the shelf that are seldom opened—maybe only to read the Christmas story, if even that? No wonder Jesus told one of the seven churches that they said they were rich, when in fact, they were destitute (Rev 3:17)!

Even with such a desire to hear God's Word, we wondered how long the children would stay on His path if they didn't get relief. Hungry and lonely children might get pulled into a lifestyle of survival that could destroy them. Certainly, each child's story pulled on our hearts.

- A beautiful six-year-old girl with a shy smile was being raised by her grandparents, along with her sister and six cousins. Her father deserted her and her family, and her mother died when she was only one. Her grandfather sometimes found work as a security guard, but it was difficult for older men to find consistent work. Her grandmother was ailing, bearing pain that made it difficult to bend over. Could we help some of the children on this homestead with their school fees and contribute to the monthly need for food?
- An eight-year-old boy was one of thirteen children. His father worked as a night guard, but he didn't make enough to feed everyone. When his mother started working in another village, the young boy and his siblings only saw her once a month. Could we help with expenses so this family could try to have more time together?
- A sixteen-year-old girl had two living parents, and her father was working, making the equivalent of $60 per month. But they were caring for ten other children, making it a challenge even to provide enough food for all those hungry mouths. Could we help this hopeful teenager reach her dreams to become a nurse and provide some relief for her family?
- A thirteen-year-old boy, one of fifteen children, was being raised by his widowed mother. His father died

when he was only eight years old. With so many children, the mother had enough help to grow maize and carry water, so they usually had something to eat. But paying tuition was impossible. The mother had a bill at the school from the preceding year, so the children weren't allowed to go back. Could we help the children in this family get an education?

- Two sisters, one ten years old and the other twelve, were being raised by their *gogo*. They were two and four when their parents died. Four other cousins also lived on this homestead, but there was no breadwinner living there. They were one of the hungriest families in the village. Could we provide food for this family and help these girls with school expenses?

Precious people back at home came through for these children, too, and we were able to do more for the kids. We started taking backpacks with us every January for the new school year. We purchased school supplies in Swaziland so we could fill each bag with what the children needed to succeed. When we realized that most of the kids lacked electricity, we bought candles and matches, then eventually oil lamps with kerosene. And every July we put together care packages with food and toiletries and a small toy.

We were eternally grateful that God continued to lead us to His servants who were willing to serve Him by serving these little ones He loved so dearly.

Luhlokohla

Also in 2013, we added the Free Evangelical Assembly at Luhlokohla. This is another rural area, with the church in the valley, but most of the children living in the surrounding mountains.

These families were extremely poor, like those in Mangcongco.

Pastor Walter Mgodlola's church provided a shining light in this village. He was an excellent leader, knowing how to train helpers and delegate responsibilities to them. It made his church solid, and they were growing.

Pastor and Mrs. Walter Mgodlola, Luhlokohla

One of the men Pastor Walter worked with and trained was Nduku Zwane. He was the Sunday school teacher, and this man had amazing organizational skills. When we visited, he had the report cards ready for every student. He also

prepared the lists of uniform sizes and colors, shoe sizes, and all the necessary school supplies. He made sure every child had written a thank you note, including a favorite Scripture and dreams for the future.

Nduku Zwane with two of our sponsored children in Luhlokohla

The children's stories unfolded, leaving us moved again to do whatever we could do to make a difference in their lives and futures.

- One boy was abandoned by his mother when he was only three years old. He lived with his *gogo*, along with four cousins. Their hut burned down, and they lost all their meager possessions. His father died when he was six years old. When he was twelve years old, he had to move in with his aunt, but he was terribly mistreated by her and her children. He ran away to find his mother, only to learn that she didn't want him. She'd been raped when she conceived him, and he was a reminder of her horror. He ran to an uncle, who helped him find his other grandmother. This young man loved to learn and had been at the top of his class, but he needed help with tuition and school fees. Could we help him make something better of his life—maybe even help make his dreams come true?

- A dear teenage girl lived with her grandparents and eleven other children. Her parents passed away. No one was working, so they struggled to find enough food. The nearest high school was too far to walk to. Could we help with school fees and also pay for her to take public transportation to give her hope of a brighter future?

- A thirteen-year-old boy and his nine-year-old sister had already said goodbye to three of their siblings who had died. There were ten children before the three passed away. This family had such a shroud of grief over them, I couldn't bear to ask what had taken the lives of the little ones. Had they starved to death? Did they have AIDS? Their father was dying with AIDS, and many in the family had also contracted the deadly disease. No one was employed, and the boy had been hearing impaired as far back as he could remember. The children were lethargic and performed badly academically. Even though elementary school was supposed to have free tuition, this family couldn't even provide the school uniforms, much less send the older children to high school. Could we help with school fees, provide some food to keep them from starving, and maybe take the boy to the ear specialist so he could have the chance to hear and succeed in school—and in life?

Again, the stories were repeated in other children at this church. At times we still felt overwhelmed, but the Lord reminded us at every turn that this was His ministry and His heart for the children.

I often re-read the words I'd written in the middle of the night—God's truths about money being just a resource, how He was calling us to things that would take a lot of it, and the much-needed reminder that it wasn't our concern, for His resources were unlimited.

And as always, He proved faithful to His Word. He continued to send beautiful supporters and donors, loving individuals and couples eager to be His vessels of love to the children. Their generosity allowed us to add blankets to the provisions for all the kids every July (Swaziland's winter). And the boy who was hearing impaired received an incredible gift from his sponsors: he had surgery on his ear to help him hear better.

For five years, we continued to expand the sponsorship program. We made four trips to Swaziland during those years, spending as much time as possible with the children to communicate their incredible worth to us, to their sponsors, and to the Lord.

We asked sponsors to get more involved by writing letters to their children and sending pictures of their families to develop a relationship with the Swazi kids. We wanted the kids to know that their sponsors weren't just sending checks; they valued the kids, prayed for them, and dreamed of a bright future for them.

We also encouraged every Swazi child to write thank you notes to their sponsors and draw pictures for them. We updated the profiles after every trip we took so the sponsors could pray more effectively for their children.

Over two hundred children had gone to school through GSM's sponsorship program by the end of 2013.

The overall outlook, however, was often discouraging. Getting an education was a chance for the children to break out of poverty, so sending them to school was a good start. But the condition of the educational system in Swaziland was pathetic. And many caregivers didn't understand the importance of letting the children study instead of serving the older relatives at night on the homesteads.

What we were doing was good, but it wasn't enough. Not nearly enough. Too many kids were being abused by their caregivers. Most were failing many subjects and needed tutored. We were concerned that they weren't making the connection between the basic necessities we provided and the love of the God who was moved with compassion for them—the One Who wanted to rescue them from injustices and pain.

We longed to show them His love. To teach them that He was good, even when their lives had been horrid. To encourage them to follow Him. And to be that involved, I needed to be in Swaziland more often.

But rare visits . . . providing mostly just school necessities . . . and from this great distance across the ocean . . . we just couldn't effectively give the children what they really needed.

We had to go deeper.

And our response to that need started with a precious little Angel.

Angel

I glanced once more around me,
and I saw with different eyes.
Renewed compassion found me
as I listened to their cries.
Smiling now, I stop to pick up
some lost mother's son.
I knew I couldn't save them all,
but I could help this one.

Excerpt from "If You Could See Them Like I See Them"

Single orphan. That's what a child in Swaziland is called when only one parent is dead.

In Angel's case, it was her father, a Mozambican, married to her Swazi mother.

Abandoned. I guess that's the word used pretty much anywhere in the world when the remaining parent dumps a child at the grandmother's house and leaves for another man.

Yeah, that's what Angel's mom did.

What does a grief-stricken, preschool-aged child think to herself when her mother doesn't stay to dry her tears?

Of course, I couldn't ask her when I met this beautiful seven-year-old.

As she timidly took her turn on the stage of The Faithful Church in the *mangwaneni,* I snapped her picture. Without a word, her shy smile captured my heart.

Thirty other children living across from Manzini's city dump also walked across that stage. Everyone's photo went into a notebook with a short bio when I got back home.

When my oldest daughter, Sara, looked through the pictures to select a child to sponsor, she was immediately drawn to Angel. She didn't tell her husband Danny which child she wanted to sponsor. But when he later browsed through the choices, he also singled out this little one. We all felt like God had specially chosen Angel for them to love, even though it would be from a distance.

When I returned to Swaziland two years later, children in the sponsorship program filled the sanctuary of the church in Manzini again, eager to say hello and get a sweet. Candy makes you popular in third world countries.

Children change a lot in two years, but one little girl looked very much like she could be "our" Angel. I asked her what her name was, and she quietly replied, "Angel."

I widened my eyes and smiled as I asked, "Angel Khosa?"

Her face lit up, and she flew into my arms and clung to me. Even when I reluctantly pulled out of her embrace, she grasped at my hand. The wonder written in her face tore me up. She wasn't merely keeping hold of my hand; she was clinging to the wonder that she was known.

Just finding out that I remembered her last name communicated to her that she was more than one more face in the crowd. She had significance.

She continued to stick close to my side the rest of the afternoon, detaching herself from holding my hand only when I needed it to take notes or photos. When I was busy with other tasks, she desperately tried to make eye contact with me, while keeping a hand on my shoulder or tugging on my shirt.

My heart was heavy when my departure neared. I knew I wouldn't see her again for another two years. Using an interpreter, I tried to assure her that Sara and Danny loved

87

her and chose her on purpose out of all the other children. Our goodbyes were teary.

In 2012, my excitement about returning to Swaziland was at an all-time high. Not only was the ministry growing with added sponsors to care for more children, but this time Sara was going with Tracy and me and two other young women, Jana Durham and Casey McMahon.

Sara could hardly wait to meet her precious Angel.

We carefully drove into the *mangwaneni*, avoiding piles of trash and navigating narrow dirt paths. We had barely passed the first few houses, when Sara suddenly cried out, "Is that Angel?"

I didn't think so; this girl seemed too old. But Sara insisted that Tracy let her out, and she threw open the van door even before we completely rolled to a stop.

She ran to the girl, calling out her name, "Angel?" The beautiful child turned in amazement, and sure enough, it was Angel, definitely looking every bit the two years older than when I'd last seen her. She recognized Sara from pictures I'd given her, and if I thought she'd clung to me before, it was nothing like this embrace the two of them shared. Sara's tears were flowing down her face in joy as she poured her love into our precious girl.

Angel with Becky's daughter,
Sara Nowlan

We found Angel's situation far different from the one I'd left two years earlier. Her mother, Bongiwe, was back in her life, being the only person available to care for her when her *gogo* died. Bongiwe had come back with another child, a boy, and since her return had also given birth to another boy. But these children had no father figure to lead them. Both of these men merely fathered children and moved on, taking no responsibility for their sons.

Bongiwe's natural maternal instincts were glaringly absent when it came to Angel. We never witnessed any physical abuse, but the apathy she displayed regarding her daughter made no sense to us. We tried to find out why, but the best explanation Pastor Sambo could give us was that possibly she had bad feelings about Angel's deceased father. I wondered if she simply had never bonded with Angel, since Bongiwe had been young when she'd left her daughter.

When we showed up with gifts for Angel and the family, Bongiwe perked up. Sara wanted to do more than just pay for school tuition, uniforms, and shoes; she bought pillows, blankets, clothes, and food to last the four of them about a month.

During our two weeks in Swaziland, we spent as much time as possible at the *mangwaneni* so Sara could give Angel the attention she so desperately craved. Angel amused herself by braiding Sara's long, blonde hair. The two of them drew pictures and wrote notes. They sang songs for each other. Angel's English had improved, so they were able to talk a lot. When they needed an interpreter, one of our Swazi friends helped out.

Angel drank in love like someone hopelessly parched. We still couldn't put our finger on exactly what was causing the distance between her and her mother. And in my ignorance, I once again assumed some of it was just a difference in our cultures.

But all of us on the team dreaded our departure. We hated to leave this precious girl in a situation where she seemed so unwanted. We managed another tearful goodbye that July.

Then in December, I received the startling news that Bongiwe had begun locking Angel out of the house—and she was only nine years old, a 3rd grader!

Bongiwe's actions communicated total rejection to Angel. And the gradual changes in the little girl's appearance convinced us that worse things were happening outside as she fended for herself in the dark. Now it appeared that men living in the squatter's camp had taken notice of our dear girl. And honestly, her deep desire for loving attention made her a prime target for their attention.

A few months later, Stan sent me a picture of Angel that he'd snapped during a visit to the church. She was wearing a wig of long dark hair and a low-cut blouse. And even more disturbing, there was a sensuality in her expression that we hadn't seen before.

Imagine the poorest part of the city with men loitering outside, laughing and drinking. Add to that the cold, hard fact that Swaziland has the highest incidence of AIDS in the world. Then throw in the myth that having sex with a virgin will cure your AIDS. And realize that after a few drinks, nobody bothers to ask whether or not a child is still a virgin.

What kind of mother puts her young daughter in a situation like that? I asked Pastor Sambo what could possibly cause Bongiwe to treat Angel with such hatred. His reply: demons.

We strongly suspected that Bongiwe was also prostituting her own child. She started purchasing nicer clothing and jewelry for both herself and Angel. And she was able to afford to move into a larger house. One she still locked Angel out of at night.

She claimed she didn't want Angel. So I searched for an orphanage or orphan home where this precious little girl could be safe . . . protected . . . loved. But even after following up on every lead, I couldn't find a spot for our precious girl.

Heart for Africa, run by Janine and Ian Maxwell, ran an excellent facility for infants up to 18 months old. And there were a few places for high schoolers. But hardly any for primary-age children. And the few available filled up quickly.

I looked for a year and a half. I sent emails and made phone calls. I visited facilities and boarding schools.

The only place willing and able to take Angel was the Catholic boarding school. But an article had just come out in the newspaper about the older lesbian girls in the school taking advantage of the younger girls.

I couldn't add to Angel's distress that way.

In January of 2014, when I returned home from another trip to Swaziland I'd made alone, I tearfully told our board of directors that there simply wasn't a spot available for Angel anywhere in the country. She was only one of thousands of children in need of care.

The board's reply was quick and sure: since we can't find a home for her, let's build her one.

Meanwhile, Sara began to raise funds to return to Swaziland with Tracy and me that July. Our dear friend Jubilee Yocum, whose graduation in Seattle originally connected us with Stan and Sue and Swaziland, had become a missionary in Mozambique. It neighbors Swaziland on the east side, and we were delighted that she was willing to meet us to help minister to our Swazi children. Sara was eager to spend time with her sweet girl, assuring Angel of her steadfast love and commitment.

But when we arrived, Pastor Sambo informed us that Angel had run away. We drove to every location where anyone suggested we might find her. Up and down city streets, slowly past stores where teenagers hung out, and through neighborhoods she'd been known to frequent. Through our tears, Sara and I realized we were going to have to give up and go back to the conference center where we were staying.

Sara's heart was broken. No matter how much she loved Angel, from such a great distance, she couldn't convince her, nor force her, to hold steady until we could help her.

Pastor Sambo found her after we left Swaziland and kept her on his homestead for a while. But since her mother lived in the *mangwaneni*, too, he felt too close to do her much good. Angel ended up bouncing around from home to home, then running off when she was tired of her environment.

Her most miserable moments were at her mother's house.

In January of 2015, I returned to Swaziland with Penny and Alley Takeda and Janie Ediger. We learned that Angel had quit attending school regularly, so she'd failed fifth grade. Pastor Sambo suggested that she might serve as a nanny to a doctor in the city of Manzini. But she had no desire to do that. We couldn't justify paying for her schooling since she refused to attend regularly—and there was no one to make sure she did.

When we met with Angel, I had to break the news to her that we weren't going to pay for her schooling. Her face fell, and her lips quivered. She seemed crushed, and maybe even a little bit like she felt we'd abandoned her.

I did my best to communicate that we wanted the best for her, but that she would also have to want it for herself—enough to do her part. We couldn't attend school in her place. Only she could build a future for herself that would get her out of the bondage of the *mangwaneni*—and her mother's neglect.

When I returned with Tracy in July, we found that she'd been more faithful in her school attendance. She was spending most of her time at her mother's, which she clearly hated. But she was positioning herself to pass.

Sara went back with me in February of 2016. To our dismay, we found that Angel continued to run off and perform badly in school. With Pastor Sambo's help, we finally arranged for Angel to live with a family near his church plant. This meant changing schools, paying new fees, buying a different uniform, and so on. But we were desperate to find a temporary answer for Angel while we raised funds to build a home.

The family who took Angel was related to the chief in that area. We promised to provide food and toiletries so her needs would be met without becoming a burden to them.

But after we left, she also ran off from this homestead, more than once. Our ministry partners searched for her and took her back each time. But everyone was growing frustrated and discouraged.

Meanwhile, I'd been working hard back at home to raise the funds to build our first care home. We were still about $20,000 short for the building itself, not to mention the furnishings we would need.

Before that trip, I hadn't told Angel of our plans to build a place where she would be wanted, a place where she could live without wondering where her basic needs would come from. I didn't want her to get excited too early, not knowing how long it would take us to complete the project. But now I wanted her to have hope so maybe she would quit running off. So I told her about the care home being built for her and other children in need of a forever family.

Everyone was concerned about what would happen to our Angel while she waited for us to help her. We could only pray that we wouldn't be too late.

Breaking a Bruised Reed

"And I will put enmity (open hostility) between you and the woman, and between your seed (offspring) and her Seed; He shall [fatally] bruise your head, and you shall [only] bruise His heel."

Genesis 3:15 AMP

Before I went to Africa, I feared snakes.

But after I walked through the slithering pit of betrayal and disillusionment, I finally climbed out of it with an unshakable awareness that God is bigger than evil.

The lesson didn't come easily.

The devil, that ancient serpent, found someone weak, someone willing to be used for his foul purposes, and he took advantage of the human vessel.

His goal was to hurt the heart of God. It wasn't difficult for the foe to devise a sinister plot designed to accomplish that. After all, God had already made it clear in His Word where His heart was: widows and fatherless children, the poor and needy of this world.

So the enemy took delight in finding ways to press hard on the bruised children, hoping to gain the added victory of closing our ministry.

We were about to be tested.

Remember my mentioning that when something in Swaziland bugged me, I was careful not to assume our western ways were right and Swazi ways were wrong? That I attributed my discomfort to cultural differences instead of any actual wrongdoing?

Well, I learned later that I should have been paying closer attention to those subtle red flags.

I didn't know then that when you're like a sheep being sent among wolves, you need to be as wary and wise as a serpent, while maintaining your innocence, as harmless and guileless as doves (Matthew 10:16).

But I was about to learn that lesson—and learn it well.

At the beginning of our ministry in Swaziland, when we worked mostly at Pastor Luendo's care home, there were only our small things nudging for attention, mostly subconsciously.

I totally missed the alert about the guys being overly hungry at our 4th of July party. I attributed their huge portions to the novelty of eating hot dogs and marshmallows—plus the party atmosphere.

But other things got my attention. Like the fact that when Pastor Luendo and his wife put on a lovely spread of food for us, the boys weren't invited into the house to eat with us.

And that I never saw the guys share any meals with the pastor's family. It bothered me. Tracy and I have four adopted children who were always included as part of the family. We never would have considered having them eat a meal separately from the rest of us.

I reasoned that perhaps the omission was only because we were company. I supposed that since there weren't enough seats for everyone to sit inside, maybe the boys were fed earlier or afterwards. Or that possibly dishes of each entrée had been taken out to them in their shack.

But when some of the boys prepared a *braai* for us (grilled meat), they didn't join us then, either. I honestly couldn't imagine that Pastor Luendo and his wife would neglect "our boys." Because I cared for these servants of the Lord, I didn't allow myself to criticize or make any judgments.

Love covers a multitude of sins, right?

My determination to walk in loving tolerance seemed noble. And in my naivete, I assumed everyone was in ministry to the children for the right reasons—a genuine love for Jesus that poured out into loving the precious children He loved.

But I was experiencing the first glimpses of a dark side of "ministry" in Swaziland. And according to what I've learned in the years since then, it's a way of life that is also common in many other African countries.

I'm going to tell you what else was going on behind the scenes—not for vindication, not out of self-righteousness, and not out of gossip.

But because we are in a spiritual battle for the lives of these children. The enemy of our souls doesn't want to merely see them bruised; he wants to break them, to crush them, to take away all hope.

The devil works in darkness; I am compelled to shine the light on how he has ravaged the children beyond the obvious incidents of poverty and abuse. With that exposure, I will also sound the battle cry and invite you to join us in prayer and spiritual warfare against the unseen forces that want to destroy them.

Something Didn't Add Up

So this is how I discovered what was taking place behind the scenes at this church care home.

It was now the summer of 2013, and I was back in Swaziland. I'd met Ashley and Philip Nelson, who felt called to serve in Africa. They wanted to visit this country to see if it might be a fit for them. I was very happy to introduce them to the people I'd come to love so dearly.

Pastor Luendo had told me that they had over 200 children eating at their feeding kitchen daily. So over a period of a couple of years, through generous donations, Grand Staff Ministries had sent $10,000 to help with food expenses.

I was eager to see the kitchen in operation. The pastor took me behind the church to give me a tour of the new structure that had been built for storing food, preparing meals, and serving the children. It was a strong building, and the children were happily receiving heaping plates of a nutritious rice/chicken dish as they made their way through a line outside the open serving window.

But despite the joy I felt from seeing hungry children eating huge portions of food, something in the back of my mind nudged for attention. I noticed boxes of food stored in the corner, and I was pretty sure I recognized them as coming from Children's Cup, a Christian organization dedicated to feeding children and teaching them about Jesus.

This time when I felt conflicted, I didn't think I should remain silent. Something was off.

So I asked the pastor if those were boxes of food provided by Children's Cup.

He quickly—maybe too quickly—assured me that yes, he was receiving food from them, but they were using the funds I'd sent to make pastries for the children every Thursday and Saturday.

He insisted that I taste one. It was a simple fried ball consisting mostly of flour, a little sugar, maybe an egg, which was deep-fried in oil that I knew they reused.

I'm certain he could tell that I wasn't my usual cheerful self as I worked the numbers mentally. Okay, yes, that was a task for me; there's a reason I taught English instead of math. But even someone numerically-challenged could figure out that it didn't take $10,000 to pay for donuts twice a week.

I also noticed that the number of children being fed wasn't even close to 200. I was becoming increasingly uneasy.

Later that day while we were interviewing sponsored children and getting pictures and biographies of potential new children to add to the sponsorship program, the pastor grew extremely agitated. He kept saying we needed to hurry. He seemed uncomfortable with the questions we asked the kids about their home life, what changes had occurred since our last visit, etc.

He had scores of additional children waiting outside for their chance to be added to the program. And he insisted on rushing us along.

Several of the original seventeen boys were missing, too. When I asked about them, the pastor became animated as he described how naughty they'd been. He accused some of them of stealing eggs.

Surprisingly, it was the boys themselves who started offering information that contradicted the facade Pastor Luendo had carefully constructed.

After the interviews, I was able to visit with one of the boys, Titus, but he looked terribly ill. He'd lost so much weight that I feared he might have HIV/AIDS. Swazis are much more reserved and private than we Americans, and I knew that, but I couldn't help myself. I grasped his arms with my hands and searched his face, repeating his name and asking him what was wrong.

He looked terrified. He tried to assure me that he was fine, but I wouldn't let him brush me off. I told him that I realized I was probably making him uncomfortable with my direct questioning, but that I absolutely had to know what was wrong so I could help.

He nervously looked behind me, repeating that he was okay. I begged him to let me take him to the doctor—promised to pay for the visit and any medications he might need.

By then Titus looked completely tortured. He couldn't quit glancing behind me, so I finally turned around, only to see Pastor Luendo glaring at Titus.

I realized then that I needed to back off, so I just made Titus promise to think about letting me take him to the doctor and to be sure to let me know if he was feeling poorly. He smiled as he thanked me, but it never reached his eyes.

Two of the missing boys, Sibusiso and Wisdom, were among those who had been accused by the pastor of stealing. According to him, they had both run off when they'd been caught.

This affected their school attendance, so I visited the headmaster of the high school. He promised that he would allow them to return if they were willing. After all, we had paid for an entire year of schooling. So I called both boys and begged them to consider going back to the care home. But neither would agree to go back.

Over the next few days, I thought back over my previous trip to Swaziland. Thando and Ndumiso had supposedly run off to their aunt's—the one who had beaten them so horribly when they were little boys. The pastor said they'd gone because they were rebellious.

Were these guys really so naughty that they would prefer going back to their abuser than to stay in a home where their needs were being met, where they were wanted? I was starting to wonder. It just didn't add up.

About twenty other children on the waiting list were also absent during this 2013 visit. The pastor had claimed that they were also rebellious, so he'd removed them from the list.

When I returned home, I questioned the pastor via email about a few things. Like why he was herding the children in like cattle, seeming to want to get as many added to the program as possible, and rushing us through the questions. I reminded him that our ministry wasn't about just sending funds; we wanted to develop relationships with the kids, showing them how valuable they are—how loved.

He responded with a message portraying how offended and hurt he was—that he was a father to these children and would never do anything to harm them. He put the emphasis back on the boys, insisting that they were being naughty. His story about them stealing eggs changed to chickens, then in another email, it was music equipment and speakers.

Exposed

During that same period, Wisdom asked to be my friend on Facebook. I learned that he had moved to South Africa. I begged him to go back to the care home and get caught up at school.

He insisted that the pastor wasn't what he seemed—that the boys weren't being fed well, that clothes donated for them were being taken to the border and sold for the pastor's benefit, that the accusations made toward the guys were false, etc.

I still couldn't imagine that the pastor was actually capable of such evil. I was pretty sure Wisdom just had sour grapes after being caught stealing. So I told him that he needed to return, humble himself, and repent of what he'd done wrong. I assured him that the pastor would forgive him and help him.

His answer chilled me.

He said he would rather die than ever set foot in that place again.

For the first time, I faced the very real possibility that Pastor Luendo's actions and lack of action went beyond the irritating or frustrating things I'd noticed—that he might actually be neglecting and abusing the boys and misusing the funds.

I didn't want to believe it. I could barely wrap my head around the possibility that a pastor, a man who seemed to preach so fervently and put on such a good show of caring compassion, was capable of this level of deception, self-serving behavior, and greed.

Colani, who was away at the university by then, was one of the young men who finally filled in the blanks about what was happening at the care home. He confirmed everything

Wisdom had told me. And he added that the guys were being forced to deceive potential sponsors. That all seventeen boys didn't really live at the care home. That blankets and clothing were staged in empty spots to make it appear that every bed was full, so the pastor could get more sponsors. That funds were not being used for the correct purposes. That instead of receiving uniforms we sent funds for, the guys had to come up with the money themselves by doing odd jobs or begging from relatives if they had any.

Colani also told me that the kitchen that we'd been told had been built for the boys was never used, except when potential donors were coming to visit. Then a pot of beans would be started on the stove, with a basket of fruit placed nicely on the table. But the guys didn't even get to eat that food. They prepared almost all of their own meals over a fire outside, consisting only of the typical ground maize, called pap or mealy meal. Only the pastor and his wife and children benefitted from the food budget that purchased vegetables, fruit, and meat.

My heart was broken at the very idea that any of this could be true. I realized that I needed to do some more research. Besides confirming Colani's and Wisdom's stories, here's what I heard repeatedly from the different boys who were no longer at the care home.

Ndumiso hadn't run away. Instead, he had been chased away in 2007 because the rabbits had gotten out of their cage while he was at church. Having nowhere else to turn, he went back to the home of the abusive aunt. The pastor had continued to collect funds for Ndumiso's care every year from 2007 to 2013, even though he didn't live at the home. The young man didn't receive one penny of help from those funds.

Titus wasn't an orphan, after all. He actually still had a mother who loved him and wanted him at home. But she'd worked for Pastor Luendo who accused her of stealing so that he could manipulate her. He insisted that Titus live at the care home, with the promise that he wouldn't turn her in to the police. He also enrolled Titus's sister in the program, forcing her to use her mother's maiden name so we and other potential donors wouldn't realize they were siblings. And he pretended that Titus' brother Chicco lived there, promising to pay his school fees if he would come to the care home when we visited so we could take his picture and update his bio. We had no idea the bio was untrue. And of course, the pastor never paid the promised school fees.

Titus finally sent me a message on Facebook in January of 2014. He admitted he was very sick, but he said it was from stomach ulcers he had from the stress of lying and deceiving people. The pastor was keeping a very close watch on everyone, fearing that the truth was starting to come out, and making every effort to control the boys who remained on the premises. Titus commented that he was probably digging his own grave by telling me any of this. He had tremendous fear of what the pastor would do to him or his family if he were caught talking to me. Yet the turmoil he felt from being part of the deception was eating him up inside, literally. He was compelled to come clean.

Pastor Luendo forced Titus to show him all his correspondence on Facebook. Then the pastor wrote a reply to me from Titus' account, pretending to be the young man. He apologized for everything he'd told me, and claimed it was all lies—that he shouldn't have ever said anything bad about the pastor who was actually like a father to him.

We waited for six months, when I returned to Swaziland in July of 2014, to hear the entire story of what had happened. Titus left the care home for an afternoon under the guise of making some exchanges in town, but he actually made his way to the Christian conference center where we were staying. He wanted me to know that he hadn't written the apology, but the pastor had. He was frightened—too much so to try to escape for good. But he was also miserable and continued to suffer from the ulcers.

Jabu was also accused by Pastor Luendo and chased away, supposedly because Jabu was 18 and had to leave, according to social welfare policies. The pastor promised to pay Jabu's tuition at the high school near his father's homestead. But it was never paid. Jabu was living alone in that area, miserable, hungry, and failing school. Here is his account of what happened before he was sent away.

Jabu

A time came when Pastor Luendo felt he could run the care centre on his own. [Pastor Kevin from Challenge Ministries Swaziland used to oversee its operation.] Pastor Kevin did not withhold permission and gave all authority to Pastor Luendo.

Before, when Pastor Kevin was still in charge, life was amazing with beautiful things. I knew that at certain times in a year there were things I would get (new school uniforms, toiletries, clothes, etc.). I was punished only for something I knew I had done wrong. Once or twice a month, I could hear words of encouragement. Everything was done accordingly and in truth. That felt like home.

When Mr. Luendo took over that care centre, there were changes that kept on being introduced which were not part of what I was told at first. What used to happen in the centre had stopped.

First, when he took over, our relationship sunk such that we guys couldn't take him as a dad anymore. We separated from staying together as a family. We were chucked out of the house where we all stayed. This meant that we had no access to watching television, no more of those family discussions.

What began to happen is we had to cook for ourselves outside. We had to go ask for food.

Sometimes we got that food after working hard. For instance, we got back from school and were hungry, because we weren't given money to buy anything to eat for lunch. So we would either go to collect firewood for the pastor's family to use, or we would fetch them water for cooking. We had to flush the toilets, clean the whole house, wash the car, water a big garden, or slash the grass. Any job that rose when we needed food was what we were obligated to do. If we failed to do that job, then we got no food.

We were bound to do these jobs because of hunger. Sometimes when we asked for food, the only thing we were given was leftovers. We had no option but to take the leftovers. Most of the time the food that we ate was terrible. Most of it was expired. And we usually could get food only after lots of arguing.

Sometimes we worked so hard, but we were starving to death. Other times the situation was worse; we could watch rain going through the place we used for cooking, and raindrops came through the top of the pot, making our fire go out. But we managed. While we went through these things, the pastor and his family ate decent food.

It was always painful to watch other students having something to eat during any short break and lunch, while I starved to death. We were never given money for buying something to eat at school. This made schooling difficult, because that introduced me to a lot of dealings in those times. I sold any of my meager belongings to anyone willing to pay a small amount—I would accept any kind of deal just to get money so I could have something to eat at school.

I do not remember at any time during those days getting a new school uniform from my sponsor. I had to hustle hard to have a good and fancy uniform to be like other students. Sometimes, winter approached only to find that I was without a jersey [jacket], and I could not think of asking anything from Mr. Luendo. I knew very well I would not get anything I asked from him and his wife.

I also wanted to be enrolled in schools around town, but that did not work out because he believed all I deserved was getting that inferior education from the local high school. He took his daughter to a good school in town that provided a good education.

Sometimes teams from America would come, and we could share our different stories, and they were touched and encouraged. They would then donate clothes for us to use, but we never knew where those clothes would end up. Sometimes we were made to go around the area and sell them and bring back the money—we were never given a quarter of it. Sometimes those clothes would be taken by people of the church.

I remember one year I had only one trouser, some t-shirts, and one pair of shoes, which I used at school. If I had a journey or anywhere to go, I could only use those things. I could not think of asking for clothes from the pastor, because I knew I would not get anything. The pastor's family dressed in fancy things.

It was amazing to see someone who stands in front of a whole congregation and tells people about God, yet that was not the life we lived all together.

I've come to realize that some people are dressed in sheepskin, while in the reality they are wolves.

What used to happen is we lived in a constructed room where one or two guys shared that room and not more than that. We slept on bunkbeds. In my case, I lived in that one room, and whenever a group of whites would come, pretty blankets were put on the extra sponges [mattresses] so that the pastor could claim that other kids slept there and more, so that funds could keep coming in.

On another note, when the whites came and wanted to have private conversations with us, we were denied talking to them. Or if we said something, it was supposed to be only good—not the bad. I was afraid to speak honestly, because I was scared to lose my education, friends, etc.

I had to pretend things were okay with me.

There are other stories from more of the boys. The pastor was mentally, emotionally, and verbally abusive. He called the boys terrible names, said they were witches, and accused them of all sorts of evil. He used his power and position to manipulate them.

Regarding money, suffice it to say that "misuse of funds" doesn't come close to what this man did. He stole money and goods intended to help orphaned children. He produced fake receipts from schools and uniform shops for many places, starting in 2012, paying the person who gave him the receipt a small fee and keeping the rest of the money for himself.

He told one of the boys that it wouldn't matter if anyone reported his theft and deception, because he had sent great sums of money into a personal account in his neighboring country of origin.

The long-lasting effect it had on these young men is still showing up today.

This man who was supposed to be their father, mentor, and pastor used them for his own financial gain. His actions affected their view of people, family, themselves, and God. He controlled them with the position of authority he held in their lives. He broke trust on every level.

He broke them.

And that's exactly the opposite of what Jesus does with bruised reeds. He never breaks them.

Spiritual abuse might be the worst kind.

I knew I couldn't turn a blind eye to this man's actions. Nor could I stay silent while monstrous deeds were being committed, all hidden behind the Name of Jesus. In January of 2014, I requested a meeting with Pastor Luendo. The chairman of his board attended the meeting at my invitation, as did two trusted friends of mine, who served as witnesses and a covering for me since Tracy couldn't make the trip.

My goal was to give him a chance to repent. When he resisted and refused to admit any wrongdoing, I asked two of the boys who had escaped to come forward to testify about what they had endured. Even more evil the pastor had engaged in was exposed, more theft of funds, deception, proof of unpaid tuitions, and more control over the boys.

His reaction to the accusations was first anger and an attempt to intimidate the boys from speaking, followed by a pathetic display of self-pity for how we were all treating him. He even threw himself down onto the floor and wept loudly at one point during the boys' testimonies. I instructed them to ignore him and continue; the chairman of his board also said through tight lips that the boys should ignore him and continue.

When the pastor's theatrics didn't get the desired result, he vacillated between pretending he was sorry and trying to intimidate me. We spent about six hours discussing the issues and giving him every opportunity to admit his wrongdoing. But he refused.

The next day he called me repeatedly, begging to meet with me again. I was speaking in Pastor Sambo's church in the *mangwaneni,* and we had a full afternoon planned with the sponsored children. But late that evening, my two friends and I met with Pastor Luendo.

He cried many tears and said he was sorry. He begged us to come for a meeting at the church. He admitted that he and his wife were both guilty. But he kept focusing on how difficult our "accusations" were making his life.

Something in my spirit cautioned me to go forward carefully. I didn't believe he was sincere. So I told him that if he was truly repentant, I needed him to do these things: 1) write down exactly what he'd done wrong, 2) ask his wife to make a written confession, 3) make a public confession and apology to his congregation with us present, and 4) also in our presence, allow our boys to make a line which he would walk down and look into their faces one by one, telling them how sorry he was for forcing them to deceive potential donors and for the terror, neglect, and abuse he'd inflicted upon them.

He promised he would do these things—anything we required so that we would keep sponsoring the children. But then he looked confused and asked us what he'd done wrong. I was shocked—did he really not understand the evil of his ways?

I reminded him that he had repeatedly misused funds/stolen, deliberately deceived potential sponsors (including me), and abused the boys in his care.

He promised to do all of the things I'd requested, and we were going to wait to receive his written confession and apology before agreeing to come to the church.

It never came. Instead he grew hateful towards us.

And to make matters worse, we couldn't find a way to continue to serve the boys who remained at the care home and the other children in that area—a total of forty-five kids in our sponsorship program.

With our Swazi friends, we brainstormed ways we might be able to help the children without going through Pastor Luendo. We even discussed it with the chairman of his board, a godly man with his heart in the right place. But going around Pastor Luendo would remove one of the four crucial elements to success: the church. Family, school, and the support from Grand Staff Ministries wouldn't be enough.

Besides, I had been warned not to set foot on the mountain at all. Friends told me to heed the warning. Other missionaries have "disappeared."

This meant we wouldn't have a way to visit with the children and update their records and pictures. I had to leave Swaziland without getting these children into school for the year.

When I got home, I waited in hopes of receiving the apology and admission of guilt I'd requested. Pastor Luendo never admitted in writing what he'd done wrong. In fact, he did just the opposite, calling a reporter from the Swazi Times newspaper to write two articles that accused donors in the States of luring the boys away from him with promises of financial help.

I was heartbroken. I'd trusted this man and his wife—trusted them to share God's love with the boys and the children in the church while we poured ourselves into helping them back in the States, working hard on fundraisers and telling everyone who would listen how great the need was. People gave because they loved God, because they had big hearts for the hurting, and because they trusted me.

Now I had to explain to our donors and sponsors why we had to put schooling on hold for their sponsored children.

I struggled with the decision to completely discontinue our service at that care center. Even in July, when Tracy and I returned to Swaziland, we asked to meet with the superintendent of the denomination Pastor Luendo served under. He graciously met with us and included another dear missionary friend in the meeting.

Both men really listened and heard our hearts. They could see that we weren't on a smear campaign against Pastor Luendo, but rather that we still hoped and prayed for his repentance. And more importantly, we eagerly desired their input to see if there was any way at all to continue to help the children in that church. We wondered if Children's Cup or some other group could help ensure the funds got to the right places.

But the missionary stated it well when he said that he knew my heart. That Grand Staff Ministries wasn't about sending a check, but rather about the relationships and discipleship of the children in the program that connected the provision of needs with the love of God. He said God's call on us wouldn't be fulfilled if we just sent the money and had some other organization facilitate payments.

He was right. So with heavy hearts, we took the news back to our board of directors, and the final decision was made to discontinue all sponsorships at Pastor Luendo's church.

Some of the sponsors switched their support to other kids on our waiting list, while others dropped out of the sponsorship program.

Meanwhile, we learned that the chairman of the board at Pastor Luendo's church had resigned.

The denomination's superintendent initiated an investigation of the pastor's actions, but the men on that committee only spoke with Pastor Luendo. None of them contacted me or any of our boys. Nothing was done to discipline him in any way.

Why did the men on the committee make light of the accusations against this pastor? I have my ideas, but I don't know for sure.

What I do know for sure is that God's Word is supposed to be our guide. Paul was clear about how the church should deal with greedy people. First he told the Corinthian church that it would be impossible to completely avoid being around anyone who is immoral, a "greedy grasper," a cheater, a thief, or an idolater. He said that you'd have to leave this world and get out of human society altogether if you hoped to stay away from everyone like that.

But when it came to the treatment of people who called themselves Christians, yet acted like that, Paul's instruction was this: don't associate with them or even eat a meal with them (1 Cor. 5:10-11).

The Bible is also clear about how we should deal with offenses. Matthew 18 explains that if a brother offends us, we should talk to him in private. If that doesn't work, we take two or three people with us to see if that will help him listen. If he still refuses to listen and do what's right, we are to take it before the church.

Why? Because if he still won't bend, the whole church is supposed to treat him just like they would treat a person who isn't even a Christian believer (Matt. 18:15-17). Which stands to reason that he shouldn't still be pastoring a Christian church or holding influence over children in need of a father figure and mentor.

I'm saddened to think that these men on the committee, who were all pastors, had the opportunity to make Pastor Luendo stop and think about the way he was living his life. Instead of calling him into account and even broadcasting his unrepentant behavior, they brushed the offenses under the rug. And he was left free to break more of Swaziland's tender bruised reeds.

One man's sin caused forty-five children to lose their support, and countless others who might have received help also lost their chance for a better future.

Besides being hurt, I was also discouraged. We'd worked so hard for every dollar, and the funds hadn't reached their intended purpose. I felt like a fool, worried that I didn't have any discernment at all. I really didn't even know how we could move forward, since I no longer knew whom I could trust in Swaziland—if anyone!

But my pain didn't even come close to the desperation this man caused our boys.

Did I hate this man? No. Paul's teaching in Ephesians 6 reminded me that people weren't the enemy. No, we struggled against unseen spiritual wickedness in high places.

In fact, I was aware that any one of us could do or say something to break one of these children. Hopefully not maliciously or purposely. But easily, without even realizing it.

I had to do some soul-searching. Had I ever lost sight of the balance of truth and love that the Swazi children needed to hear and see from me? Had I ever ignorantly put any of them in positions that left them exposed to temptation, maybe even beyond what they could bear, especially where finances were concerned? Had I ever allowed self-righteousness or pride to dictate my interactions with anyone in Swaziland?

Undoubtedly—God forgive me! I never wanted to add to their pain, even slightly—never wanted to make anything in their lives worse for them.

But somehow this pastor went far beyond unknowingly harming the boys entrusted to his care. He allowed the desire for riches and position to swallow God's call on his life. Maybe it started slowly with the intent to just take a little bit of money, but he got in too deep.

I was too tired to speculate. I just knew I hated what he'd done. I hated what his actions had done to our boys.

And I feared for his soul. Jesus said that whoever causes a little one to stumble would be better off to have a millstone tied around his neck and be plunged into the sea (Matthew 18:6).

With God's help, I forgave Pastor Luendo. I didn't see him for a long time. When we finally met, it was in a coffee shop in downtown Mbabane. He was with a white man, and I couldn't help but wonder if this man was giving the pastor finances.

I'd prayed for divine appointments that morning before leaving to run errands, and although I felt shaken, I believed God had orchestrated our being in the same place at the same time. I invited him to come to my table when he was finished visiting with the gentleman.

When he sat down, he began talking rapidly. He spent over thirty minutes telling me how difficult life had been for him after our confrontation. He described his pain in detail, saying he lost everything—good friends like us, some of "his children," and almost his mind.

He told me that it was only by God's grace that he still had his church and care center. And he claimed that during those dark days, he said he'd wondered if life was even worth living.

But he still refused to admit any wrongdoing while he emphasized the goodness of his heart since he'd forgiven us.

I felt sick. And angry. But I prayed under my breath for the Lord to help me respond.

I told him that yes, it was only by God's grace that he still had the church and care center—and I added that it was God's grace that he was even alive.

I asked Pastor Luendo to picture a hurting little girl, lying in bed at night, abused and neglected, hungry and alone and afraid. I asked him to imagine the girl crying out to God for help, asking that if He was real, He would show Himself real and bring her relief.

I then suggested that indeed, God heard her prayers and moved on me and others way across the ocean in the United States. That we were moved with compassion for the needs of that child, and we sent help in the Name of Jesus.

But as the help arrived in Swaziland, Pastor Luendo stood between the answer and the girl who had cried out to God. In fact, he even took the provisions for himself and left her in her sad condition.

And even worse, what was she to think? Maybe she decided God wasn't real. Maybe she thought He was real, but He didn't care. Or that she wasn't important enough to receive attention from Him.

I asked Pastor Luendo to consider the far-reaching effects of his actions, possibly reaching into eternity as not just one little girl, but countless children had their hope and answers snatched away from them, leaving them questioning God's goodness and love.

I reminded him of the kind of judgment that would come to anyone who caused a little one to stumble. And I told him I believed God had caused us to meet that morning because He loved him so much, He wanted him to have this warning and call to repentance.

Pastor Luendo was furious with me and began shouting, "*You* need to repent!" He kept screaming it, even with everyone gathering around us and staring. He leaned across the table, hovering over me, and finally stood up, shouting the entire time. I feared he would physically attack me, and I asked for the waitress to call the police or mall security.

Someone caught his arm and began to lead him away, and he continued to yell at me the whole way out.

Trembling, I faced the sad realization that he hadn't changed at all.

Even though our confrontation stirred up old feelings, I prayed that my words to him would become seeds that would find a place in Pastor Luendo's heart so they could grow into the fruit of true repentance.

May it be so for the sake of the many bruised children who could be still be broken by his actions.

But may it also be so for the sake of this man who still lives. Every day that he wakes up with breath in him, there is still the opportunity for him to turn around (2 Cor. 6:2).

You might be wondering how we handle the finances to ensure this doesn't happen again. First let me say that after some trial and error, including more heartache, we finally found trustworthy Swazi friends who love Jesus more than money. They have been accountable and transparent with all the financial transactions. But they are both overloaded with many ministry responsibilities that make keeping up with the record-keeping a challenge.

So in April, Grand Staff Ministries was blessed to be able to come under the umbrella of Pastor Kevin Ward's Challenge Ministries Swaziland (CMS). Besides his growing church, The Potter's Wheel, he also has care homes, sustainability projects such as purifying water and making honey, and Christian rehab for addicts. He has six accountants and three CPA's on staff, and they have graciously taken on the distribution of funds we wire to Swaziland. Their system includes many checks and balances, for which we're grateful. This has taken a huge load off our ministry partner's shoulders, and the reporting is sent to me electronically. The hard-earned dollars are now protected and make their way to the intended purposes.

The enemy hit us hard, but he didn't win. Praise God, His heart's desire for the children of Swaziland is still being met through many of God's people all over the earth.

Men of Courage

Tracy and Ndumiso

Becky's mama, Patti Belden, with Jabu

Tracy, Becky, and the Men of Courage Having Fun

Becky's mama, Patti Belden, with the Men of Courage and Patrick and Siza

Tracy with Titus

Men of Courage, August 2018
Back: Colani, Musa, Becky, Ndumiso, Sibusiso,
Jabu, George, and Menzie
Front: Titus, Thando, "Mama" Penny Takeda

Meanwhile, we had the honor of pouring into the lives of the guys who were able to escape from Pastor Luendo's abuse to start building a new life. We felt they needed a new identity, so in January of 2015, while Penny Takeda (known as Mama Penny to the guys), her daughter Ally, and my friend Janie Ediger were in Swaziland with me, during our meeting with these young men, we tossed around ideas. We all finally decided on a name that reflected how they'd come through the trauma: Men of Courage.

Men of Courage: A core group of young men who survived unthinkable spiritual abuse at the hands of a greedy pastor. They were forced to deceive potential donors, lying about the support coming in and their living conditions.

These brave fellows persevered through the hardships, trusting God instead of becoming hard in their hearts. We've watched godly character forming in them, and we are walking with them as they find their identity in Christ. Romans 5:3-5 is their motto:

> "And not only this, but [with joy] let us exult
> in our sufferings and rejoice in our hardships,
> knowing that hardship (distress, pressure,

trouble) produces patient endurance; and endurance, proven character (spiritual maturity); and proven character, hope and confident assurance [of eternal salvation]. Such hope [in God's promises] never disappoints us, because God's love has been abundantly poured out within our hearts through the Holy Spirit who was given to us."

The fact that any of these young men still love God, after what they endured by one of His supposed servants, is nothing short of miraculous.

Because we've known them for twelve years, we've watched them grow into young men, no longer our "boys." They have endured. We've watched them mature as they hope in the Lord and respond to His love. Some have been quick learners, showing gratitude for what they've received, along with a willingness to work hard to make a better future for themselves.

Others have struggled with the temptation to copy the pastor's greedy ways, using deceit and taking opportunity with available funds. They've had to learn some difficult lessons. They've been forgiven, but trust takes time to rebuild.

By God's grace, we've shown them that even when they fall, we're their family. They haven't had a frame of reference for what a healthy family looks like. Family walks with you. Family loves you enough to tell you the truth. Family doesn't step in between you and the discipline of the Lord, which comes only because He loves you so much, He wants you to learn and change. Even when He gives hard consequences, it's only because He's longing for the lesson to be learned quickly so He can restore you.

Mama Penny has been instrumental in helping several of these young men attend university or trade school and start businesses. She also often pays for dinners in restaurants to enable the Men of Courage to enjoy time with us to reinforce our sense of belonging as a family. Only heaven will reveal one day the eternal impact she has had on these young men and many other Swazi children. We will always be grateful all she's done to help finance a better future for these dearly loved guys!

"Mama" Penny Takeda and her daughter, Ally, sharing books and games with children at Shepherd's Home Care.

Two of them are married now and have beautiful daughters. We pray they will start new traditions in their families, that they will be faithful husbands and fathers so their kids have brighter futures than they had when they were growing up.

And while the young men are growing more courageous, we are growing more hopeful. In spite of overwhelming challenges from an evildoer, our God is still working to save the children of Swaziland. He's teaching us to overcome evil with good.

The devil—that ancient serpent—wanted us to give up in our relief efforts. But we were not going to quit. Instead, our board of directors determined that I should go to Swaziland more often. So we made plans for my return twice a year, enabling me to have a more accurate picture of what was happening there.

The battle wages between unseen powers of darkness and the church of Jesus Christ. But the day will come when our Savior will finally crush the evil one, and anyone who has joined his forces to take advantage of the innocent will be destroyed with him.

Meanwhile, we rejoiced at the way our God overcame the foe! He was still using His people, through Grand Staff Ministries and other organizations and individuals, to rescue children from the pit, in spite of opposition, deceit, theft, and all kinds of evil.

Yes, I still hated snakes. But Jesus Christ in us was and always would be the hope of glory (Col. 1:27). I believed that the ancient serpent and every man serving him for self-gain would come to fear the God in me—the same one Who resided in all the beautiful people He had gathered to serve the children of Swaziland with pure hands and hearts.

Would He lead me to Swazi believers who had that kind of integrity? I wanted to believe He would, but admittedly, I was not ready to let down my guard just yet.

I'd already been deceived once. I had become a bruised reed myself. My heart needed time to heal, and trust had to be restored.

So my visits to Swaziland over the next two years were spent just loving on the children, while time back in the States was spent raising funds for the care home.

And Jesus was doing His own special work in my soul, desconstructing the walls of self-protection I'd built around my heart, even while He repaired the brokenness. I was going to have to trust again before His desire to reach the Swazi children through GSM could be fulfilled.

Finding Houseparents—
Patrick and Siza Matsebula

February of 2016

It's time to give our hearts,
Bring light into the dark.
And when we trust in You,
We know that You'll come through.

Excerpt from "Can You Save Me?"

My oldest daughter, Sara, went with me to Swaziland in February of 2016. It was her third trip, but the first time she'd been there to help me get kids in school. We purchased uniforms and shoes, paid deposit slips for tuitions and school fees, and bought school supplies that we stuffed into the backpacks we'd brought with us from the States.

It left us only a few days to try to do two huge tasks: 1) find land where we could build the first care home, and 2) find suitable potential houseparents to love the children who would fill it.

I wasn't a towering woman of faith concerning these two mountains. In fact, I was completely discouraged.

Why? Because we'd been given advice that seemed utterly impossible to comply with.

There was nothing wrong with the advice. It was great. But not particularly doable.

See, we'd met this young missionary couple in the O.R. Tambo Airport while waiting for our luggage when we'd arrived in Johannesburg, South Africa. We would've missed the meeting altogether, except Sara had on a t-shirt that said Swaziland on it. That caught Anna Carmichael's eye.

She approached us to say she and her husband were missionaries in Swaziland. Even though all four of us looked like something the cat had dragged in (it's a really long flight!), we clicked.

We exchanged contact information with this attractive young couple and said we'd try to get together during our few days in Swaziland.

We were able to meet for dinner, and I picked the brains of both Anna and Ryan. Even though they were young, they'd been living in Swaziland for some time, and they had way more experience than I had.

Ryan said two things that really struck me. 1) Don't come to Swaziland with your vision and try to find someone to come alongside and make it happen. Rather, find someone in Swaziland with the vision, and you come alongside and help *them* make it happen. 2) And don't try to get a deed for land. Even if you do that, the chief still actually owns it and can take it away from you anytime he wants to. And you've already started the relationship with distrust. Rather, find a chief who will grant you the land. Just give him the obligatory cow in exchange for his generosity.

Right. Sure. After all, I've had such great success at finding people I can trust who really have the vision. (Yes, I was being facetious, even to myself.)

And hello. I've never even met a chief, much less developed the kind of relationship that would make one overjoyed to turn over land to our ministry.

And, by the way (went my musings that had now turned into a silent dialogue with God as I explained the impossibility I was facing—with more than a touch of hurt feelings toward Him), have I mentioned that I don't live in Swaziland? How am I supposed to develop those kinds of relationships when I'm only there for a few weeks twice a year?

Not to mention the fact that by the time we got the kids in school, we'd have only about five days left to even give this any attention. And I had no idea where to start. I was a little bit out of sorts—yes, even with the Lord. Because what I needed to do was so completely impossible.

During the hubbub of getting the children in school, Stan Drew mentioned to me that he knew a couple he thought we should meet: Patrick and Siza Matsebula. He said we shared a common love for orphaned children. So we arranged to meet them on a Saturday evening a few days before we had to return home.

I took an immediate liking to Patrick. He was friendly, but with a gentle strength. He had an assurance that didn't have a trace of arrogance. Everything he did and said came across with a sense of calm.

Patrick and Siza Matsebula during construction of Shepherd's Care Home

Siza was warm and bubbly, the perfect counterpart to her husband. She had a natural love for people that made us feel like we'd been friends for years.

When I asked them to share their vision, they didn't have to stop and think. Both of them had a dream for helping hurting children. In fact, they had already taken in kids who needed a place to live and financial help so they could attend school.

The dreams they shared matched exactly what we felt called to do! Even the vision of starting a church, building a preschool, feeding hungry kids—it all lined up with what we knew God wanted to do through Grand Staff Ministries.

Patrick had his laptop with him, and he pulled up the blueprints he'd drawn for building the various structures needed to care for orphaned and vulnerable children. He was trained as a building contractor!

And Siza was an experienced preschool teacher, plus a teacher of preschool teachers!

The more they talked, the more passionate they became. Sara and I gaped at them with our mouths hanging open and tears in our eyes.

While they shared their hearts, I had one of those "aha" moments of absolute clarity. The Holy Spirit reminded me of the Scripture that says, "With men, [it is] impossible, but not with God; for all things are possible with God" (Mark 10:27).

And I was watching it unfold before my very eyes.

Not only had we found a couple who had the vision and merely needed someone with the resources to make it happen, but they also had already looked at land and had favor with community leaders. The leaders had already approached the chief with the ideas, and he was interested in the proposition.

They were looking at land, even without any funding, because they were so sure God was calling them to serve children.

When I had envisioned hiring houseparents, I had in mind a couple with fewer children already in the home. The Matsebulas had five children, plus their two nieces. The nieces were older and wouldn't be staying long in the home. They were ready to attend university and find jobs. But the rest of the five children would take spaces, leaving only seven available for the needy children we were appointed to serve.

The tremendous call on this couple was evident.

Becky with Housemother Siza

I could see that even though their family would fill some of the available spaces, the Matsebulas would also make wonderful mentors to every other houseparent we eventually hired. And they could become the directors of the entire site, since we didn't yet have any long-term missionaries in Swaziland.

I was confident we should move forward to see what the Lord would do in a partnership with Patrick and Siza.

On our last Monday in Swaziland, they showed us the land they'd been considering. It was located in the village of Sipete, part of the larger area called Siphocosini. It's a rural area about a forty-minute drive from the capital.

Two people from the village gave us the tour.

An older Swazi woman who lived in the neighboring homestead hobbled over to scold us for "snooping" without permission. A few minutes later someone called one of our guides to request that we make an appearance before the chief's aunt. She'd heard we were looking around, and she wanted to know what we were up to.

I was a bit shaken. After all, I'd never been summoned to appear before royalty before. I knew from stories of our close friend Jubilee, serving in Mozambique, that we needed to go to her with a gift, not empty-handed. But I hadn't shopped for anyone with that in mind. I scrambled through the back of our rented Toyota Fortuner and realized I had some kerosene lanterns left from distributing some to the children who didn't have electricity. Good! I prayed that the Lord would somehow make them appropriate gifts.

When I presented them to the chief's aunt, He gave me the right words—I prayed that her nephew, who was the chief, and her entire family, would be a light to the people in the village forever. She got a big smile on her face.

She listened to our plans and told us she would talk to the community elders. We were dismissed.

She summoned us to a meeting with the elders two days later, which was Wednesday morning. This time I took chocolate bars for everyone, plus ink pens from Grand Staff Ministries.

We met in a round house on the chief's homestead. All of us were on the floor, segregated with the men along one part of the circle, and the women on reed mats on the other side. Patrick was the only exception, staying with me, Sara, and his wife, Siza, near the women. He interpreted for me when it was my turn to speak.

I prayed under my breath the entire time as I shared the vision for what we believed God had called us to do. We outlined the idea of the care home for children being our first priority, and we described some of the children in our sponsorship program, including Angel, who were waiting for a place to call home.

Next, we outlined the rest of the dream for a church, a preschool, a feeding program, an office, additional care homes, a place to train adults in small business enterprises, and eventually a primary school.

We were met with incredible favor as each one of the elders spoke. They were happy that we acknowledged God and His leading. They could see the benefit such a plan would be to their village. They invited Patrick to sit with them with his laptop to show the blueprints he'd drawn up for the complex.

These men promised to take the plans to the chief for his decision about whether or not to grant us the land.

When the meeting was dismissed, the older women, including the chief's aunt, got a chuckle out of my attempts to get back up from being seated on the floor for the long meeting. I hadn't used those muscles for a few years—maybe even a few decades! I finally had to roll over to my hands and knees to get up. I'm sure they considered this American a wimp! But our shared laughter was a bonding moment for us.

Now the wait began as the chief considered our proposal and request for land. Sara and I packed on Thursday, met briefly with the director of social welfare on Friday morning, and drove back to the airport in Johannesburg.

And even after we got home and continued to wait for a decision, I marveled again and again at the faithfulness of God. Not only had He caused our path to cross with Patrick and Siza's, but He had been preparing them for this calling all their lives.

Sometimes we get the idea that God uses "perfect Christian families" to produce the kinds of people who will serve Him wholeheartedly. But history and accounts in the Bible show a much different pattern.

People who have been forgiven much love Jesus more than those who think they're good enough without His grace (Luke 7:47). Out of their joyful gratitude for what He's done for them, they in turn want to lay down their lives in service to Him and others.

And many times, it's the people who have experienced loss in childhood who end up wanting to make a difference in the lives of other hurting kids.

Patrick's back story is that kind of launching pad.

My father had a total of six children with my mother. But Swaziland is a polygamous society, and my father took a second and a third wife.

The second woman was a sangoma (a witch doctor). She put curses on my mother. She also poisoned my youngest sister, who died. My mother knew this woman would kill her, too, as she had tried many times. She was always beating my mother when my father was away. Even when he knew about the mistreatment, he refused to say anything or rescue my mother. So, in desperation, she finally ran away.

I was six years old at this time, and I had one sister two years older than I was. Our father abandoned both of us, taking his second wife to live in South Africa where she pretended to heal people. My sister and I were left with no one to care for us. Our aunt, who was only seven years older than me, helped us scrounge for food to eat. We lived on wild fruits and anything we could find, day after day.

A farmer gave us a weeding job in his cotton fields so we could get money for school. Though we had aunts and uncles, they couldn't do anything to help us.

Growing up with increasing anger and bitterness in my heart, I developed a deep hatred for my father. After many years, my father returned from South Africa. By that time I was a young man, and I vowed to kill this man who had left us to starve.

One night, I hid and waylaid my father in order to kill him—determined to finally inflict justice on this man who had caused me so much sorrow. But I heard a Voice calling my name, saying I should stand up and go home. Even though I tried to ignore the Voice, it repeated a second, and then a third time. After the third calling, I responded. I knew God had prevented me from doing such a thing.

A few months later, my father searched for my mother and took her back to his home. She gave birth to three more children. My father worked in the mines in South Africa. While in that country, he took the third wife, who didn't ever bear children. But he also had a girlfriend in South Africa who bore him two children. He died working in the mines.

Thankfully, through the years, God did a healing work in my heart. I let go of the grudges against my father, and peace finally came to my soul.

As with many others who have suffered a painful childhood, Patrick ended up being a man with great compassion for hurting children. His is yet another beautiful story of redemption, as our loving Savior worked even the painful rejection in his young years for the good of countless children Patrick will love in Jesus' Name in the coming years.

And our loving Good Shepherd was ready to place His first precious little lamb, Angel, into the care of this godly man.

Praise be to God for His amazing grace!

Costly Delays

July of 2016

Your brown eyes are the highlight, starlight
Of my miserable, selfish life.
I see you workin' hard every day
Just to keep a little bit of food on your plate.

Excerpt from "Can You Save Me?"

It took us over two years to raise the funds for the first care home. But thanks to the faithfulness of many dear people, we finally broke ground in July of 2016 in the village of Sipete. The chief of Siphocosini had granted us a large plot of land in that area. Knowing it could take up to a year to complete the home, we still needed an answer for what to do for Angel in the meanwhile.

God is faithful. The Matsebulas showed their genuine concern for hurting children when they took our troubled girl into their tiny, crowded home, even before we had completed the care home.

Her grades improved dramatically under Siza's tutelage. And Angel bonded well with the family, especially the Matsebula's older nieces who took Angel under their wings.

But it wasn't all smooth sailing. Angel struggled to adjust to the constraints of living with a family. She was used to doing whatever she wanted, answering to no one. While that left her unprotected, it also gave her freedom. And that wasn't easy for her to give up.

Except possibly for the short time she lived with her *gogo*, Angel hadn't shared in normal family responsibilities, which is a big part of the Swazi culture. Everyone helps with laundry, cooking, dishes, etc. Still, Patrick and Siza patiently showed Angel the loving care she needed.

And work on the home moved forward. Tracy and I were excited to visit the site in July of 2016 to see with our own eyes how things were going. We took Linda Basler and Josh Martinson with us, and both of them connected with the Swazis early on.

Linda held babies and welcomed every woman she met into her heart. Josh helped dig the foundation, and at first the day laborers weren't sure how to take him. Josh thought perhaps they didn't appreciate him doing a job they could handle just fine—or maybe every hour he spent helping them was perceived as an hour one of them wouldn't have work to do, which would cut into their income. In his typical, humble fashion, Josh found a way to break through the distrust. By the last day we spent with these men, he had them all laughing as he mimed digging with a shovel and expressed how much he had enjoyed working alongside them.

When we returned home, all of us back in the States waited eagerly every week for updates on the building of the home. I begged for pictures and groaned when they had setbacks. The rainy season put the laborers behind schedule. The septic system collapsed and cost valuable days in redesigning and restructuring. Materials were backordered.

But the team kept moving forward!

They were determined to finish this home that would welcome Angel and other rescued girls waiting just like her.

When Hannah Ball and I made the trip to Swaziland in January of 2017, amazing progress had been made.

Window frames had been installed, and the men were plastering inside and outside.

Becky, Colani (one of our Men of Courage), and Hannah Ball

Hannah was super excited as she imagined herself living in Swaziland and spending much of her time on the site with the beautiful children God was sure to send. Both of us were encouraged and thrilled to see the home nearing completion.

Hannah Ball with a child in the mangwaneni

Finally, on April 28 2017, the Matsebulas and our sweet Angel were able to move into the completed home!

Siza and Angel pitch in to move the furniture into their new home

The move was completed one day before our annual fundraiser back at home, and we celebrated with them, sharing pictures, hugs, and happy tears on our side of the ocean. It was a dream fulfilled for everyone.

But old habits die hard. Despite Patrick's and Siza's best efforts, Angel's pattern of running off continued. Our ministry partners would look for her in her usual spots and eventually find her with various friends. Thankfully, she was always convinced to return home.

Another issue surfaced. Calling the home "Angel's Rest" proved to be a mistake. We thought the name would work, because little girls in Swaziland are often called "angels." But our Angel started telling people that it was named after her and she owned it. That she could fire the Matsebulas if she so desired. So we renamed this part of the ministry "Shepherd's Care Home."

Unfortunately, that didn't stop the trouble. Angel would get on the public transport, pretending to go to her school back in the village where the Matsebulas had lived with her before the home was completed. But instead of making it all the way to school, Angel would end up back in Manzini or hiding out with school friends. She even attended a week-long celebration once, making all of us sick with worry until a teacher finally told us where she was.

Our social worker suggested to Patrick and Siza that they might have to let Angel go if she wouldn't stay put. In fact, the woman warned that she didn't plan to let Angel return home if she ran off again. Since Angel wasn't adopted by the Matsebulas, social welfare had the final say about what course of action was chosen.

Counseling appointments were set up for Angel, but they didn't seem to make much difference.

By the time I returned to Swaziland in July of 2017, my heart was heavy over our girl. I decided to have a private chat with her. We perched side by side on the edge of the bottom bunk bed in the girls' room so we could talk uninterrupted.

I took Angel's hand and prayed for the words that might get through to her. "Angel, do you know how much I love you?"

"Yes, Mama Becky."

I continued, "Do you know how much Sara and Danny and their children love you?"

"Yes, and I love all of you, too."

"Well, honey, I'm just getting so concerned about you, because it seems like no matter how much we love you, it's not enough to really convince you to stay here where you're safe and taken care of. I'm really worried about what's going to happen to you if you keep running off."

Angel's eyebrows drew together, and she got a worried look on her face. Obviously, she wondered if she was in trouble with me.

I asked her if she was happy there in the home with the Matsebulas. If they treated her right.

She promised me that they were very good to her and she was happy there. So I asked her the obvious question: "Then why do you keep running away?"

"I miss my friends."

I knew this was true. She'd been used to hanging out with her old friends at all hours of the night and day before she went to live with the Matsebulas. And even her new friends at school lured her to spend time with them.

Angel was also accustomed to talking on her phone with friends for hours on end. To the American mind, it seemed unfathomable that a child living on her own in the *mangwaneni* or in the streets could have a phone. Even children living in mud huts without electricity often had phones, especially the teenagers. I shuddered to think what these children and our Angel had done in exchange for the phones or the airtime to use them.

But she did have a phone, and Siza had taken it away from her because she was only in seventh grade. The Matsebula children weren't allowed to have a phone until high school, and Patrick and Siza were giving Angel the same rules, which was the right thing to do.

Not to mention the fact that Angel kept breaking the rules, so they hadn't even been able to come up with a plan to reward her for good behavior.

All that meant that except for during school, she was completely cut off from the friends she loved, and for a very social young lady, that was difficult.

She complained a little bit that she never got to invite her friends over to spend time with her. I suggested that if she could go more than just a few days obeying the family rules, maybe Siza would allow her to invite someone over. She lit up.

I also proposed that if she really tried her best, I'd even ask Patrick and Siza if she could borrow a phone from one of them to talk to a friend on the weekend. I explained that it might be only for just fifteen minutes. And she might have to make the call in front of them to ensure she wasn't planning anything rebellious. Regardless, she looked overjoyed at the possibility.

Still, this wasn't the worst of our worries, and I knew I had to address the deeper concerns. "Angel, what do you want to be when you grow up?"

Her face took on a wistful expression. "I want to be a doctor."

"Do you think you will make good enough grades to be able to accomplish that dream?"

"Yes, I can do it!" she emphatically replied.

"Well, honey, do you realize that if you miss class, you won't pass? And at the end of this year, you'll have external exams that will determine whether or not you get to go to high school. Then classes become more difficult. You won't be able to catch up if you skip school to run around with your friends."

Her smile faded and she nodded her head. "I know, Mama Becky."

"Angel, do you want to get married someday and have a family?"

She brightened again. "Yes, I do," she said with a smile shining from her eyes.

"Angel, I believe you could be a wonderful wife and mother someday." I hesitated, wanting to make sure she was paying attention to my next words. "But what do you think will happen if you end up running away to meet your boyfriend and you find yourself pregnant?"

Siza had found notes she'd written to boys. And our ministry partners had often found her with guys.

"Angel, I would be so sad if you did to a baby the same thing your mother did to you."

She was silent.

"She left you with your grandmother and went on to live her own life. I hope you will never do that to a child of your own. But to change that cycle, it means you need to make wise choices. Running off isn't helping you make a good life for yourself."

I could barely hear her answer. "I know."

I desperately wanted Angel to understand the only way to see her dreams come true. Using my hands, I made an umbrella with one and shaped a stick person with my pointer finger on the other hand, standing the person under the umbrella. "Honey, I know you didn't get the protection from your mother that God intended families to enjoy. He gives kids parents as an umbrella over them to protect them from the storms of life. Their loving care gives them a safe place to live and learn and grow."

I didn't want Angel to hate her mother or judge her too harshly, so I tried to help her see that her mom probably never had the kind of protection she needed, either. That there must have been things in her life that hadn't equipped her to be the kind of mother that God wanted her to be.

The evil one, always an enemy of families, had influenced too many people in the Swazi culture away from nurturing family environments.

"I know you didn't step out from under the protective umbrella of your mother's care. Rather, you got pushed out, and the umbrella was faulty, never providing shelter from the hard things life has thrown at you." Again, I used my hands to show this happening. "That wasn't your fault. It was done to you, and you had no choice.

"But Angel, God loves you so much, He has intervened in your life to give you a chance to get what you've never had before. He's letting you live here with the Matsebulas in this beautiful home we built for you and other little girls, so that you can be part of a godly family who loves you and has your best interests at heart." I cupped a new umbrella and placed her stick figure back underneath it.

"Yes, it means that the protection comes with rules and responsibilities. You're not used to that, and you keep running out from under it. But the protection comes only when you stay there."

Knowing that often the desire to be with a boyfriend lured her away, I moved the person out from under the umbrella.

Then asked her again what would happen if she ended up pregnant.

"Has your boyfriend completed high school?"

"No."

"Does he have a job?"

"No."

"Would he be able to take care of you and pay for doctor visits and diapers and food for you and the baby?"

"No."

"Is he the kind of guy who would even stick around if you got pregnant?"

Hanging her head, Angel whispered, "No."

I held her hands in mine and pleaded with her. "God wants the best for you. I want the best for you. The Matsebulas want the best for you. But none of us can make you stay under the umbrella of protection that will provide what you need to make the best happen. Only you can do that."

I reminded her that this was her last chance. Social welfare wasn't going to let her stay if she ran off again. Angel promised she would stay put.

Our team had lots of other ministry waiting for us on that trip, including the dedication of this home our Angel called her own. We encouraged her every chance we got, and we were hopeful that she was letting our words sink in and help her change the patterns she was used to.

After we returned to the States, Angel's promise only lasted a few weeks. The next time she ran, she was gone for several days. She was finally located in a home with five kids and their *gogo*. Neighbors reported that she had been seen coming and going, leaving frequently with men in their cars.

The worst-case scenario was unfolding before our eyes; we feared she was exchanging her body for conveniences.

She had learned early in life that she could take advantage of abusive situations.

The social worker decided to give her one more chance and increased the counseling sessions. None of us could bear the thought of turning her out on her own.

We prayed that our dear girl would settle down and let love heal her heart.

In late 2017, she ran again. The police finally found her on a bus. This time they recommended that we let her go so she wouldn't influence the younger children negatively. The social worker wanted her to finish the course of counseling she was receiving. The counselor asked her to write a letter explaining why she wanted to go.

Angel wrote how much she loved being at the home and everything that had been done for her. But she claimed she wanted to move back with her family—her mom and brothers.

Of course, we knew her mother would never allow that. And Siza had also found a letter Angel had written to a boyfriend who lived in the same area as her family. It was obvious she actually just wanted to be with him and have her independence.

With heavy hearts, we allowed her to go. She was only fifteen years old.

My mama, Pattie Yates Belden, visited Swaziland with me in January of 2018. During our stop at the church in the *mangwaneni,* Angel came running to greet us, having heard we were there.

I embraced her and told her how much I loved her, as well as how sad and disappointed I was that she was no longer staying at Shepherd's Care. When Mama realized it was Angel, she rushed to our side and took this precious girl into her arms and began to weep. She told Angel how much she had loved her ever since she was a little child. She explained how many times she'd prayed over her and what high hopes she still had for her.

Angel's defenses melted away as she received the outpouring of sincere love. Love that truly wanted what was best for her. Mama continued to hold Angel, who was now also sobbing in response to such genuine affection.

Twice after that meeting, we tried to meet her again, but both times she was with friends in Mbabane, the capital of Swaziland. We couldn't arrange another time to see our precious girl.

She called a couple of times to greet me, and I was happy to hear her voice. But when she asked if we could send her to high school, I had to refuse.

I reminded Angel of the conversation I'd had with her about running away from the family God had provided for her protection and care. Sadly, I had to explain that she couldn't now have the benefits of being part of a family when she wasn't willing to come under the protective umbrella of the family.

She called me one more time, and our conversation was awkward, both of us stumbling over our words. I didn't hear from her again.

And it leaves me torn.

Part of me wants to rush in and rescue her from her own decisions.

She won't learn if I do that.

So we wait. And grieve.

And we pray. Angel has suffered the worst kind of rejection, abandonment, and abuse. Wherever she goes, we ask that she will find the grace to receive the love God longs to show her through His servants—the ones who are willing to walk with her on the path to healing and wholeness.

While we wait, we will do all we can to try to rescue other girls much sooner.

For our precious Angel, we weren't able to provide what she needed early enough.

Funding slowed us down.

May it never happen again.

Hope Fulfilled

2017 - 2018

Heaven weeps as their cries pierce the night;
I call, "Don't just hear, but do.
For in My love, I see their hearts
The same way I see you."

Excerpt from "If You Could See Them Like I See Them"

Steve Rees meeting his sponsored child, Vamsile, in July, 2017

During that same trip in July of 2017, Tracy and I finally had the privilege of dedicating Shepherd's Care Home to the Lord. Our friends Dana Siscoe and Steve Rees went with us to Swaziland for this special event. The entire village was invited to join the celebration.

Dignitaries from government offices were also invited, and we went over the list many times to ensure we hadn't left out anyone important who would take offense at our oversight.

The line-up of speakers also grew, as Patrick thought of more people who should be included: a member of the Swazi Parliament; Moses Dlamini, the director of Social Welfare; the chief of the village; the indvuna, who is the chief's right-hand man; the community leader; Patrick; and myself. I wondered how many hours the celebration would take.

We rented two large tents and borrowed folding chairs and tables for the event. Someone realized we'd also need to have a speaker and microphones, so every moment in the days leading up to the big day was full of plans and running errands.

Women from the village spent three days helping Siza prepare the food in the large kitchen of the care home. Dana and I got in on some of the fun, chopping onions and peppers, peeling potatoes and dicing them, grating home-grown red beets when they'd cooled from being boiled. Every now and then, I closed my eyes, basking in the background sounds of the women talking, laughing, and singing as we worked.

The Swazi women were so strong! They carried heavy tubs of water or vegetables on their heads and good-naturedly laughed at our feeble attempts to copy them. We didn't dare try to add a child tied to our backs, even though these women made carrying them look effortless—I knew I'd hurt myself and probably also the child and anyone in the near vicinity!

The camaraderie we felt as we worked together sealed the women's acceptance of the Matsebulas and Grand Staff Ministries into their village.

While the women stayed busy in the kitchen, Patrick had some of the men help him butcher a cow a little way from the house. With the chief and other dignitaries coming, we had to make sure we had enough meat to serve.

The day of the dedication finally arrived. The smell of the beef on the *braai* put everyone in good spirits with the expectation of a filling meal ahead.

We planned to start at 9 a.m., but only a few police officers and a handful of children were there. I was afraid people weren't going to come, after all. But typical to a Swazi event, we didn't start on time. Gradually, more people arrived. Lots of social workers came in buses to see what we'd built. Curious villagers showed up, and the tents were finally full, with extra people seated along the sides.

While we waited, Tracy and I were seated beside the chief. Someone brought strips of the beef for everyone on our row of dignitaries to enjoy before the service began. I couldn't chew the uncured meat, but it was a real treat for most.

We finally got started at almost 11 a.m. Patrick gave the dignitaries and social workers a tour of the home. Some of them commented that they would like to live there themselves!

Children from the primary school closest to the village performed traditional Swazi dances.

One of the Swazi women from the village was asked to sing a special song. She surprised me by inviting me to come forward to sing a song with her. I had the privilege of choosing the song, and I asked her to perform "Thula Sizwe" with me.

The lyrics communicated that even though life has been hard, child, don't cry; there is hope in the Lord.

The speeches inspired all of us. Moses D'Lamini especially touched me when he spoke from Acts 1:8, where Jesus told His disciples that they would receive power after the Holy Spirit came on them, and they'd be His witnesses, first in Jerusalem, then in Judea, then in Samaria, and finally into every part of the world. Mr. D'Lamini fervently declared that Shepherd's Care Home was Swaziland's Jerusalem, stating, "It begins here! It begins here!" This man's stamp of approval, as the director of Swaziland's Social Welfare, was an encouragement to the other government agencies to grant us favor, as well.

After the speeches, I was allowed to offer the prayer of dedication of the entire plot of land to the Lord, His purposes, and His glory in prayer. We invited God to continue His great work for the children of Swaziland that He loves so dearly, and His Name was lifted up!

Everyone was in a happy mood, and we all ate until we were full. Neighbors visited, and I sensed their approval. Now they'd heard why we were building in their community, and their trust seemed to go up a notch.

They proved it further by staying late into the evening to help with the cleanup. Our small team of four from the States tried to help, but they all shooed us away. I'm sure they could tell that we were too exhausted to keep up with them!

We sensed God's presence and pleasure as we drove away, praising Him for such a blessed day with our new neighbors and friends.

Now we needed our social workers to complete paper work so we could fill the empty beds with children. Our hopes were high after the dedication service, and we weren't disappointed.

Zamakhule

Zamakhule pulled her twin brother away from the barking dog of a neighbor's homestead. Even though Thabo was only a few minutes younger than her, she still felt responsible for him. He was deaf, so the dog would've been nipping at his heels before Thabo realized they were being chased.

For eleven years, Zamakhule had often watched out for Thabo, rescuing him from bullies and evil men. He knew how to communicate with her enough for the basics, but he didn't know how to determine what others were saying.

She was glad he couldn't hear what people said about their parents.

"They're drunks!"

"They're mentally ill!"

"They'll never amount to anything—and neither will their kids!"

The taunts often became more personal.

"Those kids are stupid and couldn't learn even if they ever bothered to show up at school."

"That boy is demon-possessed—that's why he can't hear!"

It hurt even more when people said that if she and Thabo were worth anything, their parents would've taken better care of them. It hurt, because she was afraid it was true.

But she never could figure out what she and Thabo had done to deserve such neglect.

Her bloated stomach growled in pain, and she nudged Thabo to keep moving. No one was home here, and the neighbor on the other side of their house had already chased them away, yelling that she didn't have enough food for her own grandchildren, so she couldn't spare any for them.

Zamakhule didn't know what to do. They were almost too weak to keep walking around the village. People there were tired of giving them handouts all the time.

But they couldn't go home—not yet. She knew her parents would still be awake, drinking and having sex without even noticing the children were in the room.

So she pulled down her tattered shirt and tried to ignore Thabo's dirty face and the smell of their unwashed bodies. Taking a deep breath, she lifted her chin and determined she wouldn't quit until they'd gotten at least a piece of bread from someone, no matter how many hours they had to wander from house to house.

It didn't matter if people liked them or approved of them. It only mattered that they ate another day.

On the day of the dedication of Shepherd's Care Home, when everyone was eating and visiting, one of the community leaders pulled me aside to discuss the twins from the village named Zamakhule and Thabo.

These eleven-year-olds were known by everyone, because they went door to door begging for food to eat. We eagerly agreed to welcome them into Shepherd's Care Home as soon as the social workers completed the paperwork.

Zamakhule had a grossly distended stomach. A physical checkup at the doctor's office revealed that she was suffering from *kwashiorkor*, a severe form of malnutrition characterized by a protein deficiency. Fluid retention causes the swelling in the abdomen. Symptoms of the disease include diarrhea, fatigue, irritability, and limited growth and cognitive development.[1] Her doctor prescribed a peanut paste that helped her begin to heal and gain weight.

She quickly became part of the family, with the Matsebula children embracing her as a sister.

A trip to the dentist brought the news that she needed not only several fillings, but also a root canal. Poor dear! I hoped she wouldn't associate pain with being part of her new family!

The infection, even after the root canal and crown, was persistent. We had hired an "auntie" to help in the house with cleaning, cooking, laundry, and care of the children. The extra help was crucial, because we knew that once the house was full, and especially after the feeding kitchen and preschool were completed and open, Siza's time would be stretched too thin.

Unfortunately, this woman wasn't particularly fond of cleaning. Worse, she wasn't particularly fond of children!

She was harsh with Zamakhule, and even tried to force her to eat with that infected area in her mouth.

I asked Siza to relieve the woman of her duties immediately. We simply couldn't have anyone working around the children who didn't share the vision for the kind of home we knew we were called to provide: a forever family where each child could experience the love of our heavenly Father through His people.

So she was out that very day, and Siza's hands were full again.

Meanwhile, we were able to get Zamakhule enrolled in the primary school closest to home. She was supposed to be in fourth grade, but she was far behind the class from missing so much school before we got her. Siza is working with her in the evenings and has her study with one of the Matsebula children, who is also in fourth grade at another school. Hopefully Zamakhule will catch up quickly now that she has stability, proper nutrition, sufficient sleep in her own bed, plenty of laughter, and lots of loving affection.

Thabo

Thabo, Zamakhule's twin brother, didn't know very many words in sign language when he became part of the family at Shepherd's Care. He didn't yet know his sign language alphabet, either, so communication was challenging.

Patrick and Siza researched where they could take sign language classes as soon as possible. They attached a poster of the sign language alphabet to the end of the entertainment center in the living room so everyone could start learning it.

Thabo didn't let a lack of words hold him back from becoming part of the family. Having a full belly, a reliable place to sleep, and plenty of kindness went a long way toward making him feel secure. And he sure was a smiley little fella! He proved to be very likeable and easy to get along with.

The Swaziland School for the Deaf is more than a two-hour drive from the home. Thabo was accepted to live there during school and come home during the three lengthy breaks.

The first time Patrick and Siza took him to school, he didn't make much of a fuss. But after spending his seven-week Christmas break from school with the family, returning to the school was more difficult for him. My mother and I were visiting Swaziland when it was time for him to go back in January of 2018, and we made the trip with them. Zamakhule was able to travel with us, as well. As we neared the school, Thabo realized where he was going, and his usual smile faded. The closer we got, the more he looked like he was going to cry.

Sure enough, as we unloaded his things, the tears started slipping out. He was in a dorm with ten other deaf boys. They managed to cheer him up a bit with their antics.

I knew only a few words in sign language, and some were a bit different in Swaziland than I'd learned in American Sign Language. But the other boys in the dorm were overjoyed that I could communicate to them, "I'm happy to see you," "Let's be friends," and by the end of the visit, the universal sign for "I love you."

Thabo seemed intrigued at the happy way these guys talked back and forth with me. I hoped it would encourage him to try harder to learn the words.

But when it became apparent that we were preparing to leave, his tears came back in full force. His dorm mom scolded him for crying. But I was moved with gratitude. Of course, not because he was sad, but because it was obvious that he had bonded with the Matsebula family. He didn't want to be separated from them, and that was a good sign.

Still, we were all heartbroken to have to leave him. We promised to come back as soon as possible.

During the rest of our Swaziland visit, we finished getting about sixty children into school, including paying their tuitions/school fees, buying their uniforms and shoes, and purchasing school supplies. Friends in the States had provided backpacks for all of them, which we had taken to Swaziland in our crammed suitcases.

We also visited homesteads, took food to needy families, prayed with caregivers, and met with our Men of Courage a couple more times. My mother had returned to the States halfway through the trip, and Penny and Ally Takeda had joined me for the second half of my stay.

One of the last things we did was to go back to the School for the Deaf to see Thabo one more time and take him a few items he needed: a bigger blanket, more toothpaste and soap, something to eat, and enough of Mama Penny's homemade cookies to share with his roommates. (She and her daughter knew how to heat up a kitchen to bless everyone around us!)

When we first arrived, another boy ran to tell Thabo he had visitors. He didn't recognize my car rental, and he was shaking his head no, that this wasn't his visitor. But then he saw me coming around the car, and he slowly smiled, searching behind me, then totally lighting up when he saw that yes, Siza was with me.

Be still, my heart! He had certainly identified with her as his new mama! We gave him the snacks and his new blanket, then distributed the cookies to all the boys in his dorm. We also handed out suckers to all the children we met until the candy ran out. Next time we'll be sure to take huge bags to share with every student.

When we left this time, there were still a few tears in Thabo's eyes, but mostly there was an earnest hope. He drank in Siza's face until the very last minute, locking eyes with her until we absolutely had to drive away. Though aching for him, my heart was at peace, because it was obvious that our sweet boy knew his family would be back to see him.

You can be surrounded by people, but still feel isolated. Especially when communication is limited by a hearing impairment. And for Thabo, being separated from his twin was also daunting, making him feel like half of himself was missing.

But love transcends language barriers. Our visit reassured Thabo that he was truly part of the Shepherd's Care family.

He and his sister weren't alone in the world anymore.

Nandi

On the 7th of February, 2018, Mama Penny, her daughter Ally, and I arrived at Shepherd's Care Home and saw that they had unexpected guests. Several social workers were seated in the living room to process the intake of a four-and-a-half-year-old girl named Nandi.

My heart immediately went out to this beautiful little girl with such huge chocolate-brown eyes. After all, she had to have had a hard start in life to end up at a care home at such a young age.

She didn't immediately want to be held by anyone. In fact, she seemed leery of all of us. Siza did a good job gaining her trust, coaxing the little one into her arms.

Penny, Ally, and I kept quiet so we wouldn't interrupt the intake, but I made an involuntary noise when Sifu, our social worker, explained why she needed care.

Nandi had been raped by her birth father.

Horrifying. But believe it or not, she is considered one of the lucky ones. She was rescued.

Incest and rape are commonplace in Swaziland.

So is pedophilia, or adults having sex with children. Some supposedly enlightened people prefer to call it "intergenerational intimacy."

But ask any of the victims. Look deeply into their eyes. You will find that changing the label doesn't lessen the pain, shame, and sense of helplessness.

And when the abuse comes from the person who is supposed to protect you and your innocence, it cuts even deeper.

Remember my early description of what I feared in Africa? Heat, monster-sized bugs, and snakes?

Well, when I learned what had happened to this sweet child, I was hot, all right—angry over the needless pain so many Swazi children were suffering.

Why isn't someone in Swaziland rising up to defend these children? Why do they remain in harmful situations for months and even years?

The reasons are multi-layered. Social workers seem to be overworked all over the globe. Swaziland is no different. Any of you who are called to this challenging line of work know that dealing with crises and abuse day after day is wearing. No matter how many times you're instructed not to become emotionally involved, you would have to be completely cold-hearted not to take some of the stories home with you at night.

But imagine the numbers of children in need of care in Swaziland. The percent of orphan-led homes alone is staggering. Many times, if the adults have all died, the chief in a village wants the children to stay there alone, simply because the property or homestead has been in the family for generations. If the child leaves, someone else will easily take the land.

In our western culture, where people move often, it's hard for us to comprehend how important land is. But in Swaziland, as in most other developing countries, it's invaluable.

That doesn't change the glaring reality that children need someone to care for them.

Alone, they're left vulnerable to rape and human trafficking, both in the sex trade and as farm workers.

Then throw in the homes where there is still an adult living on the premises—even sometimes a parent—but the child's need for protection is a low priority because of selfishness, self-centeredness, self-gratification—all sins that scream to put "me" first in every thought and action.

I've already mentioned what happens in this brutal cycle of abuse, but we can't forget the high price the children pay for the gratification of a man's base desires.

Here stood a child—a real girl, not a statistic. A four-and-a-half-year-old with a name—Nandi—and a torn body and a wounded soul.

Did Nandi already suffer from viewing her body differently? Had her self-esteem already plummeted?

Were the seeds already planted to cause her to take the path of using her body to garner favors from men? Even in elementary school, would she trade sex for a ride on the *kombi*, a van used for public transport?

God forbid, would she someday give sexual favors in exchange for airtime on her phone or a bite to eat?

How many more children—girls and boys alike—have to be ravaged before something changes?

I realize there are too many children in need, compared to the available spaces for them in care homes. But the system is almost as broken as the society. Even when our team hands over the facts of a child's abuse, and we're offering a place for the child, why on earth does it take so long to rescue her?

My heart is grieved when it seems I have to use my influence as an American to make things move forward, while our Swazi partners aren't heard. Is it wrong for me to become a dripping faucet that won't be ignored? Do we need to spend $200 an hour to hire a Swazi attorney who will move the wheels of justice to give these children a voice in the courts?

I don't have all the answers. I just know that it's not okay to ignore the cries in the night of a single child.

Nor is it okay to let finances hold us back from building as many homes as it will take to stay ahead of the children made available to us through the Swazi system. Shame on us if we come to the next stage of development on the site and we don't have the funds to move forward.

Meanwhile, here is this precious little girl who has been wounded.

Did we get Nandi in time so that her incredible value can be communicated to her enough that she believes us? We hope so.

One of the things I've always remembered from my child psychology class in college is that the ways a child views the world are almost completely set by the time she is eighteen months old, and the rest by five years of age.

We must pray fervently for miracles for Nandi and other precious children just like her. Holy Spirit, make Yourself real to these dear children. Use our willing hands and hearts to reach them with Your love.

Not tomorrow. Not someday.

Now.

Nontobeko

When my father learned that my mother was pregnant, he disappeared.

Mom had a difficult pregnancy, because she was already ill— and then abandoned to make her own way. She was unemployed and hearing impaired, so adding a baby's needs to her situation was difficult.

I've felt like a burden for as long as I can remember.

School was my one place to shine. I didn't always get to go, because even though the government changed the law to offer free tuition for elementary students, we still had to come up with some fees, a uniform, the required shoes, and school supplies.

But when I got to attend, I worked hard and paid attention in class. And I dreamed of making something out of my life. I wanted to escape from my home.

Especially in my teen years. My mother had many boyfriends coming and going from our house. She grew jealous of me when the men started paying attention to me. She also seemed to go crazy at times, suddenly beating me for no reason. She screamed at me because I made her feel old, and she thought her boyfriends would think of her that way since she had a teenage daughter.

I was almost twenty years old when I finished primary school. My mother wasn't interested in helping me pay for high school. Even if she'd wanted to, she only had a little bit of income from selling vegetables at a small roadside stand. We didn't even have enough food to eat. Attending high school would be a luxury—one we couldn't afford.

The thought of being stuck at home with my mother while my friends went on to school struck fear in my heart.

I was desperate.

One of my friends, Angel, had a sponsor through Grand Staff Ministries from the States. The pastor of the church in the mangwaneni told me they weren't taking any new sponsored children. But I begged my mother to write a note I could take to them when they visited Swaziland to get the other kids into school. I got a copy of my report card to show them that I was making good grades.

I was so afraid to ask Grand Staff Ministries for help. My whole body was shaking while I waited until all the sponsored children had taken a turn talking to Becky Spencer and her team. The pastor reminded me that I probably didn't have a chance, and I couldn't stop the tears as he motioned for me to come forward.

Even though Becky smiled at me, I couldn't stop crying. The snot was running from my nose, and I started hiccupping between my words. She had to ask me to repeat myself, because I was so upset, most of what came out of my mouth was sobbing. Finally, the pastor helped me explain my financial situation. We didn't mention how my mother treated me.

I handed Becky my mother's note and my report card. She looked so kind, but I couldn't tell what she was going to say. I continued to shiver through my tears while she read everything.

My heart dropped when Becky finally said that they weren't really taking any new sponsored children. But then she smiled again and told me that because I had good grades and obviously really wanted to go to school, they would give me a chance.

I kept crying, but now the tears were for joy. Becky warned me that this was only a trial to see if I would work hard and attend class faithfully. I promised her I would give my very best. I hoped that if I made good grades, maybe they would help me with all five years of high school.

I worked very hard during my first two years of high school. Things at home got worse, with more beatings and crazy yelling as my mother grew more jealous of me. Her boyfriends looked at me a lot, and she hated that. So did I.

She kept telling me she couldn't stand to look at me and wanted me to leave. But I just took it. I had nowhere else to go, and I was desperate to finish school. It was my only way out of the mangwaneni and away from home.

Becky visited Swaziland twice a year, and I couldn't help beaming with a huge smile every time I saw her. I was so happy to be learning! She introduced me to Patrick and Siza Matsebula, and all of us sponsored children even got to attend a party at the care home where they lived. Siza gave me and all the girls her phone number and promised she would listen anytime we needed to talk. She made us feel welcome to visit her anytime.

Grand Staff Ministries started providing my mother and me with some food every month to help me stay alive and do well in school. I was so happy to have something to eat!

During Christmas break, Siza let me stay with them at the home. I loved helping her with the little children and became close friends with her teenaged nieces. I finally opened up about what was happening at home with my mother. Siza prayed with me and even tried to talk to my mother. But mom didn't want to seem bad to anyone else. She only said she didn't want me.

When Becky came in January of 2018, I got to go with Siza to help put school supplies in the backpacks from the States. We laughed and ate candy while we worked. Becky let me pick out the backpack I wanted.

When she met with all the parents, she tried to talk to my mother, too, but mom acted like everything was fine at home. I heard Becky and Siza talking about wishing I could live in the care home, and Siza had even talked to a social worker. But no one came to check on me at home.

On February 19th, I forgot to take my clothes with me into the bathroom when I took my bath. I called out to ask my mother if she would please bring them to me. Instead she rushed into the bathroom and began beating me on my wet skin. I used my arms to cover my head, but she still managed to hit it. I was crying out for help, but no one came. She wouldn't stop, and I was afraid she was going to kill me.

I finally managed to get away from her and ran from the house without any clothes on. Neighbors were gathered around listening to the screaming, and one of them quickly let me come into her house. She gave me some clothes to put on and another neighbor then hid me from my mother.

The next morning Patrick and Siza came to pick me up so we could give a report to social welfare. We were in their office for over four hours. Finally, they said that since I was of legal age, I could live wherever I wanted.

There was no decision to make! My mother kept telling me she didn't want me—of course, I wanted to live in the care home with these people who had treated me with so much kindness!

And they seemed genuinely happy to let me become part of the family. For the first time in my life, I truly felt wanted.

This is my forever home.

When I met Nontobeko, she was crying so uncontrollably, I couldn't understand a word she was saying.

Even though we weren't officially adding any more children to our sponsorship program at the squatter's camp, I simply couldn't turn away from this girl. Something in her demeanor screamed that she was starving—not just for food, but for someone to really see her, to hear her, to notice her desperation. And to do something.

We learned that she had been Angel's best friend. But while Angel was somewhat rebellious, Nontobeko was tender. Shy. And full of grief.

Part of that moved me. The other part of it sickened me, because I knew she'd been beaten down by life to make her so reserved.

My brother's youth group sponsored her at first, then a couple we'd met through our bed and breakfast took over when the youth had to quit. When the husband lost his job, their sponsorship ended for a time. But I knew we had to keep providing for Nontobeko's education, so we raised the funds through other means.

When I met with Nontobeko and her mother, the mom tried to pretend that nothing was wrong at home, even though she had stated repeatedly that she didn't want Nontobeko to live there anymore.

I wondered if her denial was for appearance's sake, or if she just didn't want to lose the monthly food we were supplying for them.

Even though Patrick and Siza had reported the situation to social welfare, I made an attempt to appeal to the social workers one more time before I left for the States. They promised they would look into this matter. But things escalated quickly.

Just one week after I returned home from that trip, I received a message from Siza telling me that Nontobeko's situation had taken a turn for the worse.

I'm so thankful we had an open space to welcome this dear girl into the Shepherd's Care family.

And even sweeter, her former sponsor found a better job, so he and his wife are supporting her education again. There is hope for a good future for Nontobeko!

Thabisa and Nomsa

Seven-year-old Thabisa's heart pounded when she heard the key rattle in the lock of the front door. She hurried through the dark one-room house to her little sister, Nomsa, hoping to keep the four-year-old quiet when their dad burst through the door.

But she needn't have worried. Nomsa was limp, too weak to rise from the dirty foam mattress she was lying on. The girls had been out of food for days now, locked inside with no way to beg for help from a neighbor. People had quit listening to their cries a long time ago, avoiding the stench of their waste that permeated the air around their mud and stick dwelling.

Thabisa cringed at the sound of her father's footsteps. Her body went numb at the sound of his belt sliding through the loops of his pants. His abuse was worse than being alone and hungry. He slowly unzipped his pants and reached for Thabisa. She had no energy to fight back, no will to resist him when he called for her to come closer.

Didn't anyone outside the locked door know what was happening to Thabisa and Nomsa? Couldn't anyone help before he used them again?

The same day Nontobeko came to live at Shepherd's Care, these sisters were also brought to our door by social workers.

When Nomsa was a baby, their mother abandoned them.

Their father started locking them in the house when he left.

Thabisa had been raped, but it was doubtful the authorities would find enough evidence to press charges against the perpetrator. Since Nomsa has now had her fifth birthday, the doctor will examine her to see if she has also been raped.

Thabisa has never been to school, so she'll attend our preschool for a year, even though she'll be older than most of the other students. That will give her an educational foundation so she has a better chance of succeeding. Of course, Nomsa will also attend.

The little one has struggled since her arrival at Shepherd's Care. She cries a lot. At her doctor visit, she was immediately treated for a cough that she's had continually for some time. She was also given a multi-vitamin.

We didn't know these girls before they arrived at Shepherd's Care, so their adjustment is slower than it's been for some of the other children. In the photos the Matsebulas have sent to me, Thabisa seems to be adapting and responding to the rest of the family, allowing herself to smile for the pictures. But Nomsa's eyes still hold a deep sadness. She's young enough that she might not be able to communicate the source or depth of her sorrow.

We hired a new "auntie" named Thobile to help with the tasks of keeping the house and laundry clean and caring for the children. She's been amazing, so friendly and quick with her chores. She has a little girl who is almost four years old, and the smiley little gal fits right in with the children in the home.

Auntie Thobile & her daughter Mello

Auntie Thobile has been a tremendous help to Siza as everyone adjusts to the changing dynamic of new children joining the family.

Eventually social welfare will arrange for counseling for the girls, too. It takes time since the system is so broken and overloaded.

But even with help, taking in someone else's children can be overwhelming. A few days after the three new children arrived, Siza sent me a message requesting prayer. She knows I'm an adoptive mother who raised eight children, so she figured I would understand her appeal.

She was right.

What was her need? Grace. She's being stretched thin because "they all need her at once."

Oh, yes. They really do.

Lord, equip and strengthen her for the work she has been called to as a mother to the motherless.

Lindiwe

Conflicting emotions fought for preeminence as I parked our rented SUV along a dirt road during my recent trip to Swaziland. I gathered my notebook and bag, locked the car doors, and joined the rest of the team for the short walk through tall, dry grasses into Lindiwe's homestead. This was our first stop, and I feared it was also going to be the most difficult.

The hot sun bore down on us as we followed a foot path to the home. I was eager to see this sweet eleven-year-old, but I also fought dread, anger, and sadness because I knew what Lindiwe's grandfather had done to her. And now I was going to face him for the first time.

I originally met Lindiwe in July of 2014 when she was an eight-year-old second grader. She won my heart immediately with her snaggle-toothed, shy smile.

I learned that her father had abandoned her, and her mother had contracted HIV that was in full-blown AIDS. Lindiwe lived on her maternal grandparents' homestead, and her mother came and went as she pleased.

When I returned to Swaziland six months later, Lindiwe was quick to rush to my side with a ready smile and squeezy hug. She was about to start third grade, and her report card from second showed that she ranked academically at #13 of the 27 students in her class. She was happy to return to school again.

Her Sunday school teacher indicated that her attendance at church was faithful, and she also was a frequent guest at the pastor's house. This delightful little lady was well-loved by everyone around her and showed promise for a bright future.

A year later, during my visit in February of 2016, I sensed a change in her. She seemed reserved, which wasn't like her. She was now rating #9 in her class of 27 students, but something was definitely "off." She didn't even seem overly excited about starting fourth grade.

I questioned the Sunday school teacher and pastor, and they didn't know what to make of it. Of course, they were around her often, so the changes weren't as noticeable to them as they were to me—someone who saw her only a couple of times a year. I wondered aloud if her mother's illness was taking a toll on her. They offered the observation that her mother was mentally disturbed, adding that they wondered if Lindiwe might also suffer from a mental illness.

We agreed that they would keep an eye on her and try to determine what was going on in her life to bring such a change in her demeanor.

Some of the lessons I have learned in Swaziland have come at a price. Too often I have attributed things that bother me to possible cultural differences or my imagination.

But without anything concrete to go on, and having the disadvantage of not living in Swaziland, nor having our own missionaries on the ground, all I felt like I could do was ask the Sunday school teacher and the pastor, plus our two Swazi ministry partners, to try to keep an eye on her.

In January of 2017, she was ready to begin fifth grade. She had ranked #15 of 34 students at the end of fourth grade, and her average for the year was 67%. That's considered excellent in Swazi schools. Her grandmother seemed to genuinely care about her. We were providing food to the homestead on a monthly basis. And she still clung to me with big hugs every time I visited.

But her eyes lacked the sparkle that used to make them shine.

No one had any answers yet about why.

Early in the summer of that year, we had our answer to her troubled soul. The head teacher at her school told one of our ministry partners that she had finally told a teacher that her grandfather was repeatedly raping her.

It had been ongoing since third grade.

I immediately sent instructions for Patrick and Siza to take her to the hospital for an examination. They took her to a private doctor, who said that yes, it was apparent she had been raped. The hymen was broken. She had a discharge. She was bruised. Tissues were torn.

And he could tell the abuse had been happening for a long time.

Patrick and Siza contacted the police and took the doctor's report with them. Together, they all went to visit the social welfare office in that district.

Unfortunately, the worker they spoke with was offended that they hadn't come to her first. In fact, she told them that the proper procedure was to contact social welfare before anyone else.

She went on to say that they couldn't use the report from the private doctor; it had to come from the government hospital.

So this precious little girl had to endure yet another examination.

The results? This doctor claimed nothing had happened to her.

She was sent back to her grandfather's homestead.

He knew she'd told, so he started chasing her away from the home.

Her school performance slipped.

Her hope was dashed.

The social worker didn't investigate any further.

Patrick and Siza kept trying to talk to the social worker. This woman turned things against them, accusing them of trying to steal children from their families.

Frustrations were high, because even the police in that area said that everyone in the community knew what the grandpa was doing.

In an attempt to keep her safe while the wheels of justice languished, Patrick and Siza advised her to go to a neighbor's house if her grandpa was the only adult at home.

When I saw her in July of 2017, my heart overflowed with compassion. She ran into my arms and held me a very long time. I wrapped her in my arms and hugged her back, letting her stay in that safe place as long as she needed to.

I couldn't keep my tears in check. I assured her that we hadn't forgotten her, and that we would keep contacting the authorities until they did something to help her.

We had about 60 children to see during that trip, and it was a short one. This was also when we dedicated Shepherd's

Care Home, and the director of social welfare, Moses Dlamini, spoke at the service. He brought two rows of social workers with him, all seemingly impressed with our home and playfully arguing over who would get to fill the empty beds first.

But by the end of my trip, we still didn't have any answers for our precious little girl.

By January of 2018, my most recent trip, I wasn't feeling very generous toward the social workers' busy schedules, how short-staffed they were, or how they felt their hands were tied because of the differing doctor reports. In fact, I was angry, and I believe it was a holy, righteous indignation over a social injustice for this sweet girl.

One of the first things I did when I arrived was to try to set up a meeting with the director of social welfare, but Mr. Dlamini was on leave. So even though the person handling visitors at the Prime Minister's Building wasn't very accommodating, I refused to leave until I'd spoken with someone who could help me.

We finally got to visit with an experienced social worker, Mr. Makatshwa. He took lots of notes, because besides this case with Lindiwe, we also had Nontobeko's case and one concerning some twins in the *mangwaneni* who needed help from this social welfare office in Manzini. He promised to find out what was happening in these cases and get back with us.

A few days later, Mr. Makatshwa set up a meeting with me, my mother, Patrick and Siza, himself, and the social workers from this district who were supposed to report what they'd learned in their investigations.

But the women had done absolutely nothing. No calls, no visits—nothing.

I was angry and frustrated and grieved.

Angry that they'd not done their jobs.

Frustrated that the children in need of care were still waiting.

And grieved that they wouldn't even have had this meeting if I hadn't been visiting from the States. Patrick and Siza had faithfully called them, visited the office, and done the legwork to get help for all of these children. But all they'd gotten was accusations of wrongdoing instead of help for the kids.

The women promised to get busy on these cases and report back the next week. Mr. Makatshwa asked me to call him Wednesday afternoon to get a report. When I did, he still knew nothing. He promised to call me before he went to bed that night.

I never heard from him.

And he didn't answer his phone when I tried calling him twice before I departed for the United States.

From home, I sent him three messages requesting an update, but he didn't reply. Only when I mentioned hiring an attorney to take the case to the courts did I finally hear from him. He was also frustrated because the case wasn't moving forward. But the women still hadn't visited the homestead or called anyone connected to the case.

Do you want to know what haunts me?

During the meeting at the social welfare office with these women who hadn't investigated any of the three cases, he asked me what my greatest concern was for Lindiwe. Of course, I shared my obvious concern that the abuse would continue—possibly sexual, and definitely emotional and verbal—maybe also physical as punishment for her turning him in.

But worse than that? It was that after this precious little girl finally got up the nerve to tell what happened, no one had rescued her yet.

What did this communicate to her? That nobody cared? That her abuser was too big and strong to come to justice?

That she wasn't heard?

That's not okay with me.

But I'm here, back in the States, and she's there, and once again, nothing is happening since I'm not physically there as a constant source of irritation to them, nagging like a dripping faucet to try to get them to do their jobs. In all fairness, I will say the Mbabane and Bhunya offices have been far more efficient.

So why in the world is she still on that homestead when the accusations are this serious? Because the crime committed against her is commonplace in Swaziland. But that doesn't mean she shouldn't have a voice and protection!

What can we do when the authorities refuse to follow up?

Wait and pray and hope. And keep making noise.

We met with an attorney about some legal documents, and he indicated that if we need him to go to the authorities about any of the children, he knows many of the officials personally. It's possible he can get the ball rolling.

He charges $200 per hour, but it would be well worth any amount financially if we can rescue this sweet girl. Of course, the funds still have to come from somewhere.

But the issue has a lot to do with our future relationship with social welfare. We plan to build eleven more of these care homes, and most children will be placed through that organization. We need to have a good working relationship with the social workers, so I hate to burn this bridge.

But how long can we let our girl wait?

Not much longer. What if we get her as late as we got Angel? When habit patterns are already set and she isn't even capable of staying where she's loved?

And how are we supposed to act in the meanwhile?

That brings me back to my earlier comments about how visiting this homestead was the hardest one. How was I supposed to act to her abuser?

Her mother and grandmother weren't home. Only her grandfather was there keeping an eye on the children who live on this homestead. Including Lindiwe.

I knew what he'd done to her. But he was waiting for me to greet him.

I knew what I wanted to say to him. And what I wanted to do. But vengeance does not belong to me.

I cried out to God for His grace to see this man the way He sees him.

Grace was supplied. I was able to share the Good News with Lindiwe's grandfather—that no person is so filthy that the blood of Jesus can't cleanse and make him white as snow. That anyone who calls on the Name of the Lord for forgiveness of sin, welcoming Jesus into his life, will be saved.

I pray that the truth of God's Word will go deep into his heart. And that somehow, somewhere in there, a bit of good soil remains where that seed can be watered and begin to grow.

I didn't want to share Good News with this man. I wanted to call down judgment with fire on him.

But our calling isn't only to care for vulnerable children— although that is dear to God's heart.

It's also to make disciples in every nation. Teaching people to obey what God has commanded us.

Is the blood of Jesus too weak to cover even this sin? Never.

He bore every sin of every human being for all time.

I won't throw it back in His face as if it's not enough.

God have mercy on this man's soul.

But meanwhile, please, Lord, rescue our sweet Lindiwe before our window of opportunity to help her trust and heal is closed.

Tengetile

I've been working hard for as long as I can remember. I'm nine years old, the youngest child on my gogo's homestead, and a girl. So everyone expects me to do what they ask. I start the day early, before the sun lights the sky, feeding the chickens and goats, gathering eggs, hauling water, preparing breakfast for everyone, and sweeping the dirt around our house.

I also need to weed our garden and pick the vegetables. Grandma might be able to sell some of them along the road if I do a good job.

I don't remember my parents. I think I was about two years old when they died. All I've known is living with grandma. My two sisters also live here, and so do some of my cousins. Grandma is too old to work, so the church sometimes sends us a little bit of food. If they get donated clothing, we might receive something to wear. But it's never enough.

My teenaged cousin used to cry herself to sleep almost every night. We slept on the same mat, and her tears even got me wet sometimes. She missed her mother who'd abandoned her for a man. The only thing that made her happy was singing, and sometimes she came back from church with a new song to share. Her music always made me feel warm inside.

I don't usually go to church, because grandma needs my help. I'm usually late for school, too, because there are so many chores to do. When I get home from school in the afternoons, I have to hurry to gather firewood, help make supper, and take care of the older relatives. It's dark when I'm done, and there is no light for studying. I'm too tired, anyway, so I just fall onto my mat and rest a little while before I have to begin a new day's work.

I don't do very well in school, but I don't know why that matters. Nobody there likes me anyway. My cousin Mandla didn't do very well in school, either. He was a little bit older than me, and he worked hard, too. His dad was dead, and his mother also left him a long time ago. He would sometimes play with me if we got our chores done.

But both of these cousins ran away. They were tired of grandma's yelling and beatings, and they hated the long hours of work she forced on us.

That left me to face most of grandma's anger and the hard workload alone. My grades at school got worse, and I was embarrassed when the teacher told the whole class that I had last place.

But I was almost too tired to care. I was always hungry, always sad, and lonely even with family members around me. Life didn't seem worth living.

I wish this was an unusual story, but it's very common for grandparents or aunts and uncles to turn children into slaves when the parents die or abandon them. Instead of being cherished and wanted as dearly loved family members, they are valued only for what they can produce through working.

When I first met Tengetile, she always looked at the floor and had a darkness about her. No smiles. Mostly fear, like you'd see in a dog that had been beaten harshly by its owner.

We quickly determined that her situation warranted our providing monthly food for this homestead.

Tengetile was always late to our sponsorship meetings, and her grandmother never attended—nor did she attend church. Tengitile's church attendance was sporadic and falling off even more. I finally requested a meeting with the grandmother and asked the pastor to remind her that our sponsorship came with certain requirements, including faithful church attendance.

When the grandmother came to talk with me, I brought up Tengetile's tardiness at school and poor grades. I hinted at knowing how hard the little girl was working, and the grandmother quickly blamed other family members for demanding that she wait on them hand and foot. She suddenly became Tengetile's rescuer, eager to stand against injustice. I didn't press the issue or let her know that I was well aware who was overworking the girl. Instead, I was thankful that maybe now things would get better at home.

I emphasized that if Tengetile's grades didn't improve, we wouldn't be able to keep her in the sponsorship program.

I also reminded her that church attendance wasn't optional for our sponsored children. Neither were our meetings with the kids when I visited Swaziland. She agreed to allow Tengetile to attend church on a regular basis, and she also gave her permission to come to the wiener roast party we were hosting at the church.

Tengetile showed up for the party in her best clothes. She played mostly alone, but she did have a lot of fun learning to use the hoola hoop we'd brought and eating all the marshmallows she could hold. It was a happy day for her, and she bonded with me in a new way. I'd never seen her so happy.

Her joy lasted even into my next couple of visits. The *gogo* informed us that she'd contacted a social worker because Tengetile wanted to live at Shepherd's Care Home. The social worker in that area had approved the move, and we were overjoyed!

But the joy was short-lived. The social worker was incorrect, because an investigation had to be conducted first, and they always try to find a relative willing to take the child. Even though Tengetile's relatives had communicated that they didn't want the responsibility and expenses of her care, social welfare pressed for this unsatisfactory solution.

We'll wait and pray. And as soon as funds are available, we'll build more care homes so we have space for children like Tengetile who just need to be shown that they are valued, not for what they can do, but for who they are.

How Jesus Does Justice

Why do we question God's Holy Word
When He told us to into go into all the world?
When we should really be askin' Him
If we have enough true passion.

Excerpt from "Can You Save Me?"

I love the end of the verse from Isaiah 42:3: "A bruised reed He will not break, and a dimly burning wick He will not quench; *He will bring forth justice in truth*" (italics mine).

How does Jesus bring forth justice for these children?

How does His truth make that justice possible?

Think back on the countless Bible stories that tell of the ways He tenderly cared for people who were damaged. How he brought encouragement for those who were about to give up hope.

Did He berate them or toss them into the dung heap? Never!

When we look at those stories from His Word, we see His heart for people suffering from injustice. Because He is the same yesterday, today, and forever, we can rest assured that He will extend the same justice toward us (Heb. 13:8). Let's look at a few examples and the way truth kept these bruised people from being completely broken.

Hannah

Hannah was a Hebrew woman who was childless. Adding insult to injury, her husband's other wife provoked her, wanting to rub it in, to irritate and embarrass her about her empty arms.

But the Lord heard her earnest plea as she knelt at the temple, asking God to look at her suffering and remember her with a son. He sent her a message through the priest, Eli, saying He would grant her petition.

She not only gave birth to Samuel, who became a great prophet in Israel, but she also gave birth to three more sons and two daughters after that. The truth was, God had a good plan for Hannah. He did more with her barrenness, surrendered to Him, than what was ever accomplished with her rival's fruitful womb (1 Sam. 1-3).

Joseph

Do you think Joseph ever felt like a bruised reed? Did he fear that his hope of having his God-given dreams come to pass would be snuffed out forever?

His own brothers, jealous of the favor shown by their father to him, sought to take his life, but then sold him into slavery instead. Potiphar's wife lied about him, resulting in his imprisonment. Pharaoh's cupbearer, a prisoner who was released, forgot about him for two years after promising to speak well of him when being freed.

Joseph was battered by mistreatment and unfair judgments. Surely, he was tempted to give up on the dreams he thought had come from God.

Yet God never forgot His call on Joseph's life. Eventually the Lord freed him and brought vindication and justice his way. He didn't allow the suffering to break Joseph or snuff out his life—or his dreams. Truth prevailed—the truth that God really did have a plan for his life, one that would save His people. And everything that happened to Joseph made him more suited to that call on his life (Gen. 37, 39-41).

The Woman Caught in Adultery

Remember the woman caught in adultery, accused alone instead of with the man who was also entangled in her sheets? She was hated, judged, and guilty, deserving of the pending death the religious leaders waited to inflict on her.

This was a woman bruised and despairing, exposed with no excuse. But instead of facing the stones, she received mercy from Jesus as He extended hope that she could be a changed woman with a changed life. Every person ready to judge her was also guilty before Him, and when Jesus helped them realize that, they left and went home. Then when He withheld deserved condemnation of this woman, with the pardon He gave her the desire to live a new, sin-free life (John 8:1-11). She experienced the freeing truth that she wasn't chained to her old life; love and grace had the power to transform her.

The Father with a
Demon-Possessed Son

There's the amazing story of the man whose son was demon-possessed. The evil spirit had such horrible control over this child. It made him unable to speak. It would seize him and throw him down—sometimes trying to burn him up in fire or drown him in water. It caused the boy to foam at the mouth, grind his teeth, and become stiff.

This dad was exhausted and fearful for his boy. He asked Jesus to help if He could. Jesus' response was quick. *If He could?* Oh, yes, He could! "All things are possible for the one who believes and trusts [in Me]!" (Mark 9:23 AMP).

The father cried out desperately, his words piercing the air, saying "I do believe; help [me overcome] my unbelief" (Mark 9:24 AMP).

Although the man admitted that he had only a little faith, Jesus didn't rebuke him for that. Rather, He moved on the faith that man *did* have. His son was healed and completely restored.

The truth was, the man didn't have to have perfect faith for Jesus to help him. God doesn't quench what faith we have; He shows *Himself* faithful, causing *our* faith to grow. The truth is, Jesus loves to set people free from oppression! We don't have to try to talk Him into it.

The Mother with a Demon-Possessed Daughter

Think of the Syrophoenician woman with a demon-possessed daughter. This woman fell at Jesus' feet, pleading with Him to drive the demon out of her girl. He told her that the children of Israel should be fed first, and that their bread shouldn't be thrown to the "pet dogs" or non-Jews.

This mother could have lost hope right then. But she pressed in with the truth that moved His hand of healing: even the dogs under the table get some crumbs. And glory to God, a crumb from the Lord is more than enough to bring healing!

This mama was persistent for the sake of her dear child. And Jesus was certainly not going to crush her hopes. He was impressed with her humility and faith, and He granted her request. When she got home, she found her daughter relaxed and resting, completely free from the demon (Mark 7:25-30).

Christ's Compassion

All five of these stories show us God's character by the way He responded to each situation. Our dear Swazi children need the same kind of hope He offered them. Some feel overlooked, like Hannah. Some seem to have their dreams blocked at every turn, like Joseph. Some are stained with guilt, like the woman caught in adultery. Some believe, but are also afraid their faith is not enough, like the father of the demon-possessed boy. And some feel like outcasts, treated like they're unworthy, like the mother of the demon-possessed girl.

Jesus had a soft spot for people who were hurting, ready to give up.

"When He saw the crowds, He was moved with compassion and pity for them, because they were dispirited and distressed, like sheep without a shepherd. Then He said to His disciples, 'The harvest is [indeed] plentiful, but the workers are few. So pray to the Lord of the harvest to send out workers into His harvest'" (Matthew 9:36-38 AMP).

Right after that command, He sent out the twelve to do exactly that—to go as workers into the harvest, preaching the Good News of His kingdom, freely giving what they had received from Him (Matthew 10:1-8).

We must let Him do justice through us in exactly the same ways. As we share the Good News—true, new messages to our Swazi children—we counteract the lies that have been used against them. And it's crucial that we follow up those truths with actions that speak as loudly as our words.

Raped children are convinced that they are dirty, used up, guilty, unwanted, only an object, and worthless. These are lies from the pit of hell. The truth is, they aren't responsible for the tragic events that harmed them. They still have so much to offer in this world. They are cherished and loved, not only by God, but also by us. They are worth the life of God's own Son!

Abandoned children feel the sting of rejection while their parents chase a new love instead of caring for them. They believe they have little or no worth. The truth is, they are wanted and worth more than riches.

So we show up and tell them repeatedly that they are loved and valued. Then we follow our words up with practical provisions of their daily needs and with relationships built over time, confirming our words by our actions. When we give of our wealth, we place high value on these children.

Every injustice throughout history has been reversed only when people have been willing to speak truth and take action, empowered by God for the task.

Our name, Grand Staff Ministries, comes from an awareness that these vulnerable, abandoned, and orphaned children in Swaziland are like little lost lambs. The Good Shepherd's staff is grand enough—great enough—to meet every need.

But He does it through people. People like you and me.

He has raised us up and equipped us with such wealth in this world. Our Father longs for us to answer the needs with the awareness that we are here for such a time as this.

We provide the physical needs with our resources, and we provide the accompanying relationships that show the children their great value and the Savior's unending love. Our Swazi houseparents, Patrick and Siza, are crucial in the restoration efforts. So are our Swazi ministry partners, Nduku and Mpendulo. They are on the ground, physically meeting needs every day.

But the people here in the States are just as important to the big picture. Without our giving, the ministry taking place in Swaziland can't go forward.

Remember that there was a time when I didn't know God wanted to use me to rescue His precious Swazi children. Maybe like me, you didn't know you wanted to make a difference in their lives. But now you've heard of the needs and God's heart for these children. We need an entire army of people willing to let the Good Shepherd use us to take care of His little lambs.

You matter. No one else can do what the Lord is calling *you* to do.

Our God gives beauty for ashes. Hope for despair. This doesn't happen overnight; it happens over time, as we consistently show up and let our Savior "show off." Not arrogantly, but with His mighty love and power that find expression in restoring souls.

Reeds are used to make baskets. Let every bruised reed, every precious child we serve in Swaziland, become a vessel the Lord Jesus can use as something beautiful and glorious.

Reeds can also be used to make flutes. They are inexpensive, so normally when they're broken, another one can be made easily. But occasionally, a musician becomes fond of the sound or feel of a particular flute, so he's willing to repair the broken one. A flute through which he can continue to make beautiful music.

In fact, the Hebrew word for reed is *ganeh*. A flute made from reed can also be called a *ganeh*. It's a beautiful play on words, because it is the same word used to mean "to redeem."[2] When our precious children in Swaziland are bruised reeds, our Savior won't break them. No, he will redeem them instead, even playing beautiful music through their redeemed lives.

That's my prayer.

And it's my mission.

Will you join me?

How Jesus Does Rewards

I had a dream I saw heaven;
And there were people gathered round.
They seemed to be expecting something special,
And in their hands, each one held a crown.

I watched as Jesus made His way through the crowds;
He gently touched the first man on the head.
He smiled as they locked eyes, and He looked kinda proud;
I listened close, and this is what He said,

"Well done, good and faithful one;
You can enter my rest.
Well done, my devoted son;
Your sacrifice has been blessed!

My joy is now complete in you,
And every tear has been wiped away;
Everything you've given is now given back to you;
Just look into my eyes and hear me say, 'Well done.'"

The man was puzzled and he told the Lord,
"I can't imagine what I could have done
To be receiving these sweet welcome home words."
Then Jesus said, "Come look at this, my son."

The years flashed back, we saw the times he'd stopped to pray;
We watched so many hungry people fed;
He'd clothed the naked, called the lost, none was turned away,
Then Jesus cried, "I meant it when I said,

'Well done, good and faithful one;
You can enter my rest.
Well done, my devoted son;
Your sacrifice has been blessed!
My joy is now complete in you,
And every tear has been wiped away;

Everything you've given is now given back to you;
Just look into my eyes and hear me say,
'Well done.'"

The man was broken, and he fell to his knees;
He placed his shining crown at Jesus' feet.
He whispered, "My reward is simply knowing you are pleased,
And you have helped me serve the least of these."
Jesus said, "You did it all to me!"

"Well Done" Dedicated to Becky's Uncle Bobby and Aunt Mary
Warnock at their retirement from service in the Salvation Army,
January 15, 2005.

Have you ever imagined what Judgment Day will look like?

What emotions does that image bring up in you? Joyful anticipation? Guilt? Fear?

Many of us grow uncomfortable when we consider what Jesus will say to us on that day.

He described the conversation in vivid terms in Matthew 25:31-46 when talking to His disciples shortly before His crucifixion:

> When the Son of Man comes in His glory (His majesty and splendor), and all the holy angels with Him, then He will sit on the throne of His glory.
> All nations will be gathered before Him, and He will separate them [the people] from one another as a shepherd separates his sheep from the goats; And He will cause the sheep to stand at His right hand, but the goats at His left. Then the King will say to those at His right hand,

"Come, you blessed of My Father [you favored of God and appointed to eternal salvation], inherit (receive as your own) the kingdom prepared for you from the foundation of the world.

For I was hungry and you gave Me food, I was thirsty and you gave Me something to drink, I was a stranger and you brought Me together with yourselves and welcomed and entertained and lodged Me, I was naked and you clothed Me, I was sick and you visited Me with help and ministering care, I was in prison and you came to see Me."

Then the just and upright will answer Him, "Lord, when did we see You hungry and gave You food, or thirsty and gave You something to drink? And when did we see You a stranger and welcomed and entertained You, or naked and clothed You? And when did we see You sick or in prison and came to visit You?"

And the King will reply to them, "Truly I tell you, in so far as you did it for one of the least [in the estimation of men] of these My brethren, you did it for Me."

Then He will say to those at His left hand, "Begone from Me, you cursed, into the eternal fire prepared for the devil and his angels! For I was hungry and you gave Me no food, I was thirsty and you gave Me nothing to drink, I was a stranger and you did not welcome Me and entertain Me, I was naked and you did not clothe Me, I was sick and in prison and you did not visit Me with help and ministering care."

Then they also [in their turn] will answer, "Lord, when did we see You hungry or thirsty or a stranger or naked or sick or in prison, and did not minister to You?"

And He will reply to them, "Solemnly I declare to you, in so far as you failed to do it for the least [in the estimation of men] of these, you failed to do it for Me."

Then they will go away into eternal punishment, but those who are just and upright and in right standing with God into eternal life.

Wow. That's pretty straightforward.

And I don't see anything in there about merely praying the sinner's prayer. Rather, it's very clear here that anyone who has genuinely done that and has started a new life with God will, of course, have also taken on service to Him by loving other people.

Notice that there isn't anything in the list about teaching at a Christian school, leading worship at church, teaching children's church, helping with youth group, or teaching adult Sunday school—all of which I was doing in 1990, the first time this portion of Scripture pierced my heart.

Don't get me wrong—all of these things are important. When we first tell God in prayer that we know we're sinners and need His salvation, we start our journey with Him. But it's only the beginning.

And those other activities are necessary to keep a church functioning and people growing in their faith.

But everything I was doing was inward to the church, and nothing was outward to a hurting world. Both are crucial to the heart of God. The first (church ministry) is for the believer's growth and equipping to do the second (reaching the lost).

The Role of Works

Let's be clear from the start: we don't earn our salvation by our works. It is the gift of God, by faith through grace (Eph. 2:8-9). Jesus did all of the work for this one. It's impossible for us to be good enough to earn our salvation. In fact, we have all earned a death sentence, because we have all sinned (Rom. 6:23).

But He paid the sentence for everyone who will receive His gift (Rom. 3:23). Indescribable!

Yet sadly, too often we've been taught that receiving that gift is the end of the story, when it's actually supposed to launch our new direction in life.

Imagine opening a Christmas gift and being all excited about getting exactly what you most wanted or needed, only to put it on the top shelf of your closet. Maybe you take it down and admire it from time to time, but you never use it.

Ridiculous! Yet we all have received the best Christmas gift ever, in the truest sense of the word. And we seem content to just take it down now and then—maybe even once a week when we go to worship service—then put it back on the shelf until next time.

Salvation is meant to be only the first step in a lifetime journey of faith with Jesus.

And His intent is that our salvation will show up in the way we spend our resources: our time, our energy, and our money.

Again, we don't work in order to gain salvation. Just the opposite is true. If we've received salvation, it is supposed to be evident by the way we live or work. In other words, we work *because* we have gained salvation.

I recently heard Joyce Meyer read this quote from a book by David Windham: "There's truth to the old saying that the entry fee into Christianity is completely free. But the annual subscription is everything that you've got. No one will be in the coming Kingdom on the basis of his or her own achievements, but only on the basis of God's generosity. But everyone will be called to account on the Day of Judgment and will be rewarded according to his or her response to the Lord's generosity."[3]

In fact, when Jesus addressed the seven spirits of the seven churches in Revelation 2 and 3, He let each of them know that He was aware of their deeds—their works—what they were or weren't doing.

And all except one of the seven churches were warned of pending consequences if they didn't make changes.

Most Bible scholars believe that these messages probably applied to three sets of people: 1) actual churches that existed at the time John wrote them down, 2) certain types of churches and individuals, and 3) church ages, with the last one most clearly describing the church that exists right before Jesus returns.

That's the Laodicean church (Revelation 3:14-22).

Before Jesus describes this group of people, He first describes Himself. He calls Himself the Amen, which means the "so be it." He says He is the trusted and faithful and true Witness, even the source or origin of the beginning of everything. In other words, He's seen it all since the very day He created the world and mankind.

Then He informs the people in this church that He knows their deeds. And He describes their work as neither cold nor hot.

I love the Amplified Bible, because it adds English words to better describe what was meant in the original Greek text: "I know your deeds, that you are neither cold (invigorating, refreshing) nor hot (healing, therapeutic); I wish that you were cold or hot. So because you are lukewarm (spiritually useless), and neither cold nor hot, I will vomit you out of My mouth (rejecting you with disgust)" (Rev. 3:15-16 AMP).

Then He describes the people in more detail: "Because you say, 'I am rich, and have prospered and grown wealthy, and have need of nothing,' and you do not know that you are wretched and miserable and poor and blind and naked [without hope and in great need], I counsel you to buy from Me gold that has been heated red hot and refined by fire so that you may become truly rich; and white clothes [representing righteousness] to clothe yourself so that the shame of your nakedness will not be seen; and healing salve to put on your eyes so that you may see" (Rev. 3:17-18 AMP).

Jesus wasn't trying to shame these folks into more service. Rather, He was trying to save them from shame later on when He would have to come to either reward or correct them.

In fact, in the next few verses, He explains that He rebukes and disciplines those He dearly and tenderly loves. He shows us our faults and instructs us, so we have the chance to change. He encourages us to be "enthusiastic" in our repentance, changing not only the outward behavior, but the inner self, the old way of thinking. He entreats us to stop our sinful behavior—for that's what selfish and indulgent behavior is—and rather seek God's will.

What good is our accumulated wealth if we aren't doing anything eternal with it? We must do more than merely make ourselves comfortable.

In fact, if our deeds/works aren't bringing life—inspiring the saved and refreshing the weary, healing the broken and restoring the sick—then we're as lost as they are.

God says that rich people who hoard it all for themselves disgust Him, even to the point of rejecting them!

How can we go to church and only take in more, more, more to make ourselves comfortable, and then convince ourselves that we're just fine because we say we love God and we're dedicated?

He says otherwise! He wants us to see our true condition—to buy salve for our eyes from Him. Not so we'll feel condemned and guilty, but rather so that we'll see our true condition and turn it around to please Him.

Paul warned early believers that people who crave riches fall into temptation and traps, even ruin and destruction. He said that rich people should avoid being arrogant, that they shouldn't put their trust in riches, because wealth is uncertain. He charged rich people to be generous in sharing what they had, which would lay up treasures for them in heaven, where their treasure would endure forever (1 Tim. 6:9, 17-19).

Defining "Rich"

Wait, you might be thinking, "I'm not rich. I barely make it from paycheck to paycheck."

But let's pause to consider the facts. According to Richard Stearns in his book *The Hole in Our Gospel*, there are plenty of startling statistics.[4]

"If your income is $25,000 per year, you are wealthier than approximately 90% of the world's population. If you make $50,000 per year, you are wealthier than 99% of the world!"

Ninety-three percent of people in the world don't own a car.

Just 1% of the income of the American church is $65,000,000. Just a little bit more than that amount would lift the poorest one billion people in the world out of extreme poverty.

We're the wealthiest nation of Christians in the world. Do we tithe, which is giving 10% of our income to the Lord and His work? No. Only about 5% of American households tithe. That number improves to about 12% of households who claim to be born-again Christians. And even of the evangelical Christians who claim their faith has the greatest influence on their life and conduct, still only about 24% of them tithe.

If all church-goers in America tithed, we would have an additional $500 billion for service every year.

Yet Americans typically spend:

- $897 billion on entertainment
- $18 billion on photography
- $42 billion on sports and recreational vehicles
- $25 billion on revenues of lotteries
- $42 billion in foreign assistance for the world
- $67 billion on pets
- $10 billion on cosmetic surgery

Is being rich a sin? No—God caused many of His people to become wealthy with His blessings on their lives and crops and flocks.

And in Matthew 25, right before the parable of Jesus separating the sheep from the goats, He tells the story of people stewarding talents of gold. The two who increased what they were responsible for, for the sake of their Master, were blessed with even more.

God just cares a lot more about what we *do* with our money than how much of it we have.

The Link Between Our Works and Our Rewards

In the very last chapter of the Bible, in one of the very last things Jesus said in His written Word, we find this promise: "Behold, I (Jesus) am coming quickly, and My reward is with Me, to give to each one according to the merit of his deeds (earthly works, faithfulness)" (Rev. 22:12).

Quickly is an interesting choice of words. Especially when we consider that it's been about 2,000 years since He said it!

But what if quickly means suddenly? What if, as we read in Luke 21:34-35, He's talking about how we need to be on guard, not distracted or weighed down with self-indulgence and worries, because He will return suddenly.

He describes His return like a trap for those who aren't paying attention! Picture an animal padding through the woods, not realizing it's about to step into the steel jaws of capture.

What if He's warning us to be ready, like when He described the ten virgins, half of whom were prepared for the bridegroom's arrival, and half who were not (Matt.25:1-13).

Let's be honest. Good intentions don't count when the Lord starts tallying up the rewards He will give His people.

Maybe we're so tired, so overworked and stressed, we don't really care whether or not we have any rewards waiting for us on Judgment Day. We might just be glad that we're saved, even if we don't have any special recognition from God to savor for eternity.

But dear ones, we will care on that day.

One of my favorite movies is *Schindler's List*, starring Liam Neeson in the part of Oskar Schindler. It's the true story of a greedy Czech businessman who is transformed during the Holocaust. He plans to get rich from the war, opening a factory in German-occupied Poland. But he ends up penniless after turning his factory into a refuge, rescuing about 1,100 Jews from being gassed at the Auschwitz camp.

At the end of the movie after a radio announcement that Germany has surrendered, he is surrounded by the factory workers whose lives have been saved by his sacrifices. He is preparing to leave, knowing he will likely be hunted and arrested for being a member of the Nazi party and a profiteer from slave labor.

Before he goes, the workers present him with a gold ring they fashioned from melting down the gold from someone's tooth. The inscription they've chosen is a Hebrew expression from the Talmud: "Whoever saves one life saves the world entire." Oskar tearfully slips the ring onto his finger, then states several times, "I could have got more." He says he threw away so much money.

He approaches his car and realizes he could've saved ten more people if he'd sold it. He pulls the gold pin from his lapel, finally seeing that at least one more life could've been saved if he'd sold it—maybe two. He is finally seeing his possessions in light of the real people who were waiting to be rescued. His transformation is evident by the regret he expresses—not for a fortune lost, but for the lives he could've spared, but didn't.

Oh, friends, at the end of this life, when our opportunities to serve are over, the way we've lived will matter! Will we rejoice because the Lord has been willing to use us in His Kingdom on earth, giving us the great privilege of laying down our lives in service to others? Or will we have regrets for how little we did in His Name?

We won't be satisfied if we just barely get into heaven by the skin of our teeth! First Corinthians 3 describes that as being saved, but like someone who has gone through a fire and gotten scorched by it, barely managing to survive.

It's kind of ironic that someone who lives only for self in this life, putting comfort and convenience before the Kingdom of God, will think that he won't mind if he misses out on rewards that will affect him forever.

He will care. And it will be too late to change the outcome.

Why do so many nonprofits and churches struggle to find enough help? The causes of these ministries are valid and good. And people intend to pitch in.

Just at our ministry thrift boutique alone, we've had over 120 people indicate that they're interested in volunteering at the store. We send a monthly reminder of what is happening in Swaziland and when we need help. So why do we have a core group of only fifteen regular, committed volunteers?

Because service is never convenient. It requires sacrifice. It's often messy and tiring—and it interferes with other things we'd like to be doing. Not to mention that it involves putting up with other people who are often overworked and stressed! (Ha-ha, isn't that an effective appeal for help?)

Dear brothers and sisters, the Swazi kids aren't the only ones who need to be convinced they are loved. We all need to hear it, feel it, see it, and be consumed by the kind of love that wraps us in warm welcome.

We can't give what we don't have. And none of us needs one more thing on our to-do list—or one more thing to feel guilty about when we aren't participating in serving.

But loving others isn't meant to be drudgery or a burden. It's meant to be life to us—letting God live in us, and through us, so that we can then spread the beauty of His goodness, forgiveness, and love.

Our motives matter. We don't serve to impress others. We're just called to be sheep, serving Jesus by serving those He loves. We fill up with His love, and we let it spill out of us. Like rivers of living water that flow from deep within us, out to a hurting world (John 7:38).

When Jesus described the two things that would fulfill the entire law of God, He said it was loving God first, then loving our neighbors like we love ourselves.

When we love Him, we love what He loves. We hate what He hates. We are moved with compassion for what touches His heart.

He planned long ago all the good things He intended for us to do. Ephesians 2:10 reads, "For we are God's [own] handiwork (His workmanship), recreated in Christ Jesus, [born anew] that we may do those good works which God predestined (planned beforehand) for us [taking paths which He prepared ahead of time], that we should walk in them [living the good life which He prearranged and made ready for us to live]."

Our work will look different from person to person. The Lord has given us varying gifts that work well in specific jobs. And He positions us where He wants to use us so that everyone has the opportunity to experience His love.

Every now and then someone gets agitated and tells me that they think we ought to be taking care of the needy people right here in the United States. It's true that Jesus told His disciples to be witnesses first in Jerusalem (their hometown). And if we don't know how to serve at home, then we probably won't really do much elsewhere.

But He also said that the Gospel message would grow until it reached the uttermost parts of the world. In fact, He *commanded* His disciples to take on that task, sharing His message everywhere (Matt. 28:19; Acts 1:8).

Most people associate me with Grand Staff Ministries, because I'm the vocal one who is out in front where people see me. My husband Tracy is behind the scenes, rarely speaking up and certainly never planning an event or recruiting volunteers or donors. His gift is helping, and he is much happier doing that quietly in the shadows.

But over thirty years ago, the Lord sent Tracy a message through John Hollar, who is now the president of Christ for the Nations. He is a man of God we respect greatly, and he and his wife Ann were in our home for a Bible study. He told Tracy that he would be a father to many more children than we could see at that time.

Tracy and I found that interesting, because we had two birth children and one on the way. We also had two teenage girls living with us, and they were part of our family for three years. Five kids seemed like a lot of children at the time.

Of course, we couldn't have known then that over a decade later, God would call us to adopt a sibling group of four children whose birth dad had killed their mother. Nor that we would have another baby a few years later!

We figured that message from God had been fulfilled with eight children and the two girls thrown in for a total of ten.

But God wasn't done yet. All along, in His heart and plans, He already had planned "beforehand," as we read earlier in Ephesians 2, the good work Tracy was called to do. And he's been an amazing father figure to "our boys" who now comprise the Men of Courage. Only eternity will show the impact this quiet man has made as he's laid down his life to help fundraise, be Mr. Fix-it at the boutique, use his vacation time to go to Swaziland, and show by example that working with your hands is a noble profession.

Without our even knowing it, God was teaching Tracy how to serve first at home, then stretching him a bit further to adopt children from outside of the family, and finally to serve the kids in Swaziland. He's my hero.

Honestly, there are many needs all over the globe. But here in the United States, we have government programs and church outreaches to almost anyone who is willing to receive the help. We have such abundance that even many people receiving services here would be considered wealthy in third world countries.

Should we begrudge the help going into those corners of the world, where the cries of the people reach heaven every day? Where God hears and is moved with compassion to send the answer?

Some people look at the suffering around the world and ask why a good God would allow it. But He is asking why *we* allow it. He is willing and even very much desiring that the needs are met. But He uses people.

Serving the needs of others is much simpler than we make it. It's the Golden Rule. In other words, if we truly love those around us, we begin to treat them the way we would want to be treated. And Jesus went a step further, saying we should love them like He loves them—which is equivalent to treating them like He would treat them (John 13:34).

Mothers and fathers, grandmothers and grandfathers, we start loving someone else's little ones the way we love our own.

What lengths would we go to if one of our own children or grandchildren were hungry? If one had been raped? If one had been abandoned or had contracted AIDS or had never been to the doctor or dentist? If one couldn't afford to go to school?

We would do anything—everything in our power to make sure that child's needs were met.

And love compels us to do the exact same thing for the precious Swazi children Jesus loves so dearly.

In fact, He said that if we love *Him*, we'll take care of *them*.

We can't take care of all of them. But I have a feeling that together, we can take care of many more of them who are waiting to see God's love up close, in practical ways that convince them He is real and good and willing to meet their needs.

And every time we give or go or do, Jesus says we're serving Him.

Do we know what His rewards will be? Scripture doesn't give us much of a picture. I can imagine the huge thanks waiting for Patrick and Siza for laying down their lives every day in direct service to the children.

But I can also imagine what's waiting for some of our widows and retired people and moms and teens and even children who volunteer at the thrift boutique. It's sometimes hard to remember that standing for hours steaming wrinkled clothing so it sells better, or sorting through donations, or cleaning dishes, or running the cash register is connected just as much to meeting the needs of the children as when Siza quiets a child after a nightmare or Patrick makes another trip to the doctor's office or the older kids help prepare a meal for the new girl who was just placed in the home.

God sees it all. Even if no one else does.

And we can be sure that the God who created this amazing earth we live on surely won't skimp while He's preparing our eternal home and rewards.

And through all eternity, we'll never regret what we've given to "the least of these" in His Name.

Looking Ahead

You've read about our plans to build additional care homes for the children, and that's critically important for those who need rescued. It's equally important to meet the needs of people in the immediate neighborhood—the village of Sipete in Siphocosini, Swaziland. The chief granted us a beautiful plot of land with ample space that will allow us to develop additional services as funds become available. Please read on to dream with me and catch God's vision for the care center.

The Feeding Program

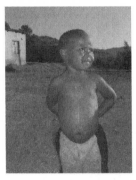

Homestead child—from the look of his bloated belly, he's obviously suffering from malnutrition

Building a feeding kitchen and preschool was the best project to take on after the first care home was completed. As I type this, we're just days away from opening.

We'll provide meals to village children who aren't eligible to live in the care homes but who still need to supplement their food source. We're working with an organization that has already screened people in the community. This way we'll ensure the truly hungry children are served.

This isn't the "Swazi" way. They would typically feed any child in the village, regardless of income level and need.

But we've learned through our own experience, from our reading, and from what we've gleaned from other organizations, that our efforts to help can sometimes actually hurt people. We aren't called to do for them what they can do for themselves. (See the suggested reading list in the back if you're interested in learning from others' experience in this area, especially *Toxic Charity* and *When Helping Hurts*.)

The fact is, every dollar spent feeding a child whose family can afford to feed him, is food taken out of the mouth of a child who has no one providing that basic need.

We're eager to get started, knowing what an incredible difference the food will make for every child in the program. And if we have enough donors, we will be able to feed every hungry child in the village of Sipete.

The food will do more than provide nutrition and energy to the kids. It will also protect many from the desperate decision to sell their bodies in exchange for food. Besides the emotional, mental, and spiritual toll this takes on a child, it obviously also greatly increases the risk of contracting HIV/AIDS.

Along with the meals, we'll also provide food for the soul and spirit.

Our ministry partners will play games with the children and develop relationships with them. They'll share a Bible story and have activities and crafts for the kids to help them remember the scriptural truths.

Giving children the opportunity to interact with loving, mature believers will change their lives. If the kids have been on their own or caring for sick parents, they probably haven't enjoyed the benefits of Bible stories and prayers. At the feeding kitchen, some of that will be remedied.

Nduku and Mpendulo,
our ministry partners

Two or three women from the community will serve as volunteers to cook for the children and serve the food. These women will not be paid for their help, but they will be supplied with food to take home to their families.

The Preschool

Little Lambs Christian Preschool will be open to any child in the village between the ages of four and seven. The first phase is two classrooms that will enable us to teach up to forty children. If both of those classrooms are consistently full, and there is a need for additional classrooms, we have space to add more rooms as funds become available.

We will charge tuition to ensure we can always pay our teachers and purchase supplies. If a family is unable to pay the full tuition, as sponsors commit to helping, we can offer a full or partial scholarship.

We're extremely excited about the quality foundation this will lay for the little ones who attend. They will learn to speak English, which will give them a head start in primary school. Little Lambs will thrive under Siza's capable leadership.

The Church

Good Shepherd's Church currently meets in the living room of the care home. Patrick and Siza are both graduates of the Swaziland College of Theology, having earned diplomas in Bible theology. Once the feeding kitchen opens, the congregation will start meeting in the dining area. We've furnished the kitchen with folding tables so they can be moved in and out to make more space as the church grows.

It's been a joy to watch the Matsebulas reach out to individuals in the community. They have a full living room every Sunday, with many children from the village drawn to the love of Jesus they experience through this family.

Siza leads the worship, and Patrick brings the messages. Their children are also active, helping with the singing and making the children from the village feel welcome.

The Next Project:
A Grand Staff Ministries Office

Although in some ways it might seem crucial to start on the next care home as soon as possible, we know that an office is a must. Patrick and Siza have stacks of paperwork in their bedroom, and the office tasks have grown beyond their ability to keep up with everything.

We need detailed files on every child, every employee, every receipt, and so on. All of those files need to be . . . well, filed!

We also need a secretary who can track the calendar for us. For instance, paying attention to when it's time to do an evaluation on an employee. Or when it's time to take a child back for a medical checkup.

We need a person who can enter data and turn in requisitions for materials. Someone to handle emails and correspondence. Someone to take minutes at team meetings. Someone who can take applications for the preschool. And someone who can answer a myriad of questions. Because until we have an office with a secretary, everyone seeking information about any aspect of the ministry will have to interrupt class to get information from Siza.

In other words, we need an office furnished with files, a computer, brochures describing services we offer, and a people person who is also a great organizer!

The plan is to make this a two-story building. The first floor will have a reception area for the secretary, an office for Patrick to use as the director of GSM Swaziland and our site manager, and a conference room where meetings and trainings can take place.

Then on the second floor, we'll build a small living area which could be used for long-term missionaries, visiting short-term missionaries, or live-in help. It's a good use of the area to build up, as it reduces costs and takes up less space than constructing living quarters in a separate building.

God loves for everything to be done decently and in order. Having an administrative assistant who can keep things organized and on time is a huge need—and will be an equally huge blessing. We're already praising Him for the people

He'll move on to catch this part of the vision and help see it through to fruition.

This building project is a necessary part of the foundation of excellence and organization for every other aspect of our ministry on the site.

Sustainability Projects

One of our goals is to ensure that every child in the care homes, at the feeding kitchen, and in the preschool always has something to eat.

We will grow many of our own crops, eventually replacing much of what we purchase with what we've grown ourselves. We have our first crop in the ground, and Sibusiso (one of our Men of Courage) has been hired to help with planting, weeding, etc.

We also have indigenous chickens that will reproduce and provide meat. Eventually we will add more chickens, both layers and fryers, to provide eggs and meat.

The goal will be to have enough of both products to sell, providing the funds to buy more seed and plants for the gardens and to purchase food we can't grow. If our crops succeed and our chickens thrive, eventually the income will also allow us to purchase other items needed in the homes.

In addition, we want to add livestock to provide milk, starting with goats. Geoff and Liz D'Urso donated funds for the fencing, and The Center, a Foursquare Church in Wichita, Kansas, pastored by David and Marla Beeson, donated funds to purchase five goats. Both couples are dear friends to Tracy and me. Having friends come alongside as part of the team humbles us. We're so honored to serve Jesus together!

We'd love to experiment with growing coffee on the site, with hopes of eventually roasting it and selling it in Swaziland and in the States as a fundraiser. Currently we purchase coffee in South Africa, and it sells well here at home. But if we can produce our own, the income will be greater.

I've taken Patrick and Siza to visit two sustainability farms in Swaziland, and we've learned a lot from what's already being done there. Everyone is excited about the willingness of these other farmers to give ongoing advice while we're learning how to proceed.

More Care Homes

The orphanage model from the last century has housed many children, and many hundreds of thousands of children have found shelter. But we believe that God has called us at Grand Staff Ministries to show vulnerable and orphaned children in Swaziland the Father's love more directly through a home environment with houseparents, serving up to twelve children per home.

Some will worry that we can't reach as many children if we only have twelve in each home. And that's a valid concern. But we believe as we show these children how valued they are—as we make them part of a family unit—they will grow in ways that can't be realized in a more institutionalized environment.

Every ministry and nonprofit has to discover what I like to call their particular ministry "DNA." Some feel called to reach as many as possible (quantity), while others know they're called to go deeper with each individual child (quality). Both are valid. At Grand Staff Ministries, we believe we are called to provide a family/discipleship model.

So we'll build one house at a time and get it staffed and filled with children before building the next one.

The long-term plan is to build eleven more care homes. Each one will house between eight and twelve children. The size will depend on whether or not we've got houseparents with both a father and a mother, or if we have only the mother. A couple can manage more children than one person can.

We will use Swazi houseparents who know the language and understand the culture.

It's challenging to find couples who are monogamous, who love and follow Jesus, and who are willing to love someone else's children like their own. For one thing, even the young men who are dedicated disciples of Jesus often don't have enough income to marry. Many haven't finished high school, or when they complete Form 5, they can't afford to attend university. And without that training, it's challenging to find employment that will enable the man to provide for a family.

We're trusting the Lord, who sent Patrick and Siza to us at exactly the right time, to also send us godly, loving parents for the next set of children.

We believe . . . we hope . . . and we pray that the children in our care will heal and become part of the solution for the future of Swaziland.

The Primary School

I'm a former teacher. I taught elementary music and junior high English and history back in the days before it was called middle school.

Education is a big deal to me. It's a tool to equip people to not only make a living, but also to fulfill their calling in this world.

When we first started our sponsorship program, we had no idea how challenged the Swaziland school system was.

We asked the children to bring us their report cards so we could make sure they were learning.

I'll never forget the day I looked at the first one, seated across from a primary (elementary) young man. The first thing I noticed on his report was that he was #4 in his class of 31 students. Immediately I began to praise him for that achievement, and his grin let his white teeth shine against his beautiful black skin.

But I'm so readable, he had to notice the way my own smile morphed into near horror as I continued to read through his results.

He had failed more than half of his subjects!

I studied the report for several minutes and asked our ministry partner to help me decipher it. Surely there had been a mistake! How could he be #4 in the class if he'd failed so miserably?

But I was interpreting the results correctly. I was completely distraught. If #4 looked like this, what did the report card for the thirty-first child look like?

It was my first glimpse of how broken the Swazi schools were—and still are. And closer inspection proved that being first in the class doesn't mean all A's—it might even mean having some C's, D's, E's, and F's. Ending up with an average of 65% or higher is to be applauded. Forget striving for a 4.0; rising to the top can happen even with a lot of failure.

Of course, I wanted to know what was wrong that caused such poor results. The answer is multi-faceted, and every return trip to Swaziland has given me another piece of the puzzle:

- Many of the children go to school without any food to eat. Some schools serve a lunch, but it is given to the kids several hours after they've been in class. The brain can't function without fuel—brain cells need food so that they can work like they're designed to work. Hungry kids don't learn well.
- Many of the children are late to class because of the tasks they need to accomplish before they leave home. Some are caring for sick parents. Others have grandmothers who expect them to work in the fields, haul water, do laundry, sweep or rake the dirt outside the home to keep snakes away, or a host of other jobs.
- In the mountainous areas, it gets dark around 4:30 p.m. during the winter. Most of the kids have to gather firewood and complete other after-school tasks when they get home in the late afternoon. Since many of the homesteads are without electricity, it's a challenge for the children to do their homework in the evenings. Because it's dark, most Swazis go to bed early, and usually they don't have separate sleeping quarters. The kids simply can't keep the rest of the household awake while they study. Which ties in with the next point:
- Many of the caregivers, especially the grandmothers, haven't completed school, and they just don't see the value in it. So it's not a priority. Survival is. They aren't able to make the connection between an education and a brighter future.

- Children in rural areas often live too far away from the nearest school to make it feasible to attend. School attendance isn't compulsory in Swaziland.
- Too often, children don't have textbooks. It's pretty hard to do your homework or study if you don't even have the book. GSM pays book fees, so we were shocked to learn that it didn't ensure having the books to take home.
- Some classes have sixty or more students in them, with only one teacher and no aide. It's impossible for one teacher to be able to meet the vastly different academic needs of every student.
- Children who are being abused have difficulty paying attention in class. This includes a huge majority of the students. Add to that children whose parents have abandoned them for a new "love" or kids who are taking care of sick relatives who are going to die. Life situations run through their minds instead of addition and subtraction or identifying nouns and verbs.
- Many teachers in the primary schools failed Form 5, which is the final year of high school. We just recently learned that there is a college (of sorts) with the main focus of training these young adults to teach the young students. How can they teach what they don't know? Answer: they can't, and they aren't.

So what are we doing about it? We've tried buying candles and kerosene lamps so the children can see to study on winter nights. We've tried various tutoring programs. We've given pep talks to the children and caregivers alike, encouraging them to make time for studying. We've started purchasing textbooks and passing them down to the next kids every year.

But it's not enough.

We need a place to give the children an excellent academic foundation. This will give them an advantage when it comes to finding employment that provides more than just survival income, starting their own successful businesses, getting into the university or trade school, and equipping them for whatever God has called them to do in life.

Of course, receiving a post-secondary education can seem insurmountable because of the expense. But some of the sponsors are willing to pay the tuition, and the government has a scholarship program for high-performing students. The government scholarship doesn't cover 100% of the fees, but it certainly brings down the cost. Our elementary school will make a difference by laying a solid foundation educationally and spiritually, so we send off children who are ready to take leadership in their country.

We were overjoyed to learn that the chief in Siphocosini granted us additional land so we can build a primary school. The two families who own the land were incredibly gracious to release it for this purpose. So as soon as possible, we need to begin this project. We hope and pray that the funds will be provided quickly enough to allow us to have the school ready in the next two years so that our preschoolers can go straight into first grade right here on-site. This has a chance of happening if we build classrooms for one or two grades at a time and gradually add on as the students move through those grades.

Our vision is to provide a Christian education with the best teachers possible. This will mean finding willing educators in the States who will come, and training up great educators in Swaziland. It will mean finding a qualified headmaster who will hold a standard of excellence, bringing every subject back to the Word of God and His ways.

It will also mean we will need many more sponsors for individual students who will attend the school.

The kind of school we envision will provide hope to many Swazi children who will receive a superior education, along with learning what it means to follow Jesus as they study, hear God's Word interwoven into every subject, and watch the lives of their godly teachers.

And it will position these students to receive the greatly sought-after government scholarships.

It's a worthwhile vision, and we trust that the Father is already sending His call to many of His people, even now, before the blueprint has even been drawn.

What we do to raise funds— and how you can help:

Grand Staff Thrift
Boutique
215 North Main
Buhler, KS 67522
Hours:
Tuesday – Saturday
10a.m. – 5 p.m.

For a couple of years, our board of directors discussed various ways we could produce ongoing monthly income. We knew it would be an important part of the vision for the care center coming to pass. We would need enough funds to pay our houseparents, hire housekeepers and gardeners, provide food for the children, take them to the doctor and dentist, and so on.

Even though we planned to keep the sponsorship program for children living in the home, not every sponsor would be able to afford to cover all of the expenses.

So it was obvious we couldn't commit to caring for lots of children unless we had a strong monthly income stream.

The idea of opening a thrift store was tossed around from time to time, and as we got closer to our goal of having the funds to break ground on the care home, we knew we had to make some decisions. I started looking at available retail space, and various friends accompanied me to visit thrift stores and boutiques in our area.

We finally made the decision to open a thrift boutique in our little town of Buhler. Not every small town would be a suitable choice for such a store, but Buhler is already a destination shopping location. Vicky Adrian, owner of Adrian's Unique Boutique, has done a fantastic job bringing people to Buhler, even from surrounding states.

So the customer flow was already here. But to ensure we would appeal to her shoppers, we'd need to make it a thrift boutique, not just a thrift store. That would require careful sorting of donations and appealing displays.

It was risky. One board member quit her term early because she was afraid we'd fail and be stuck holding the bills.

We got the key to our store on August 31, 2015. And we worked like crazy to be open in about a month—October 2, 2015! That was the weekend of Buhler Frolic, a major annual celebration. Lots of people come "home" for school reunions and visiting family. And what a wonderful first weekend!

Since then, we've been absolutely amazed by the things people donate. Excellent quality, name-brand clothing and housewares, beautiful décor that's still in style, and many items that are new with tags dangling from them. Even enough antique or vintage items to warrant their own space.

We've also been blown away by the loyalty of our customers and the way so many new people continue to find us. Folks are driving from cities several hours away—they love our store, our prices, and our stuff that much! And most of all, what the proceeds accomplish!

Paula Wiens (left) & Janie Ediger getting goofy with donations!

Becky Spellman sorting clothes

Equally as important, we've been impressed and blessed by our team of volunteers. God has faithfully moved on the hearts of a key group of mostly women who give of themselves regularly to sort and price items, clean donations, steam clothes, make displays, and so on. They are the backbone of the store and a huge part of the reason we've succeeded. (Even our store manager, Paula Wiens, is a volunteer, sent by God.)

We've expanded from two side-by-side connected buildings, to a third huge room (also connected) that includes three smaller retail rooms, a breakroom and another large workroom. Honestly, we have so many donations, we could use an additional big room.

Ardyth Tolle steaming jeans

Faye Spencer was selected by the boutique manager and other leaders as the 2018 Volunteer of the Year for her faithful service. She stands and steams clothes at least twice a week, no matter how much pain she's in. Thank you, Faye—you're an example to us all!

We've had enough proceeds from the store to meet the monthly obligations in Swaziland and to contribute heavily to the building of the feeding kitchen/preschool.

Rod Tolle painting furniture

As we expand in Swaziland, so will the monthly expenses, which is why we also need dedicated monthly sponsors/donors. But for now, the boutique is providing a huge chunk of what's needed, and we're grateful.

I love it when new customers walk in the front door and look around slightly confused, saying, "Oh, I thought this was the thrift store." I chuckle and assure them they're in the right place. Their reply is, "Oh—it doesn't look like a thrift store." Then there's a pause, and some add, "It doesn't smell like a thrift store, either!" Yes! Mission accomplished!

Truly, this boutique was an idea birthed in heaven. We praise God for leading us the way He has. It does take lots of hands to make it work, and we have jobs for almost anyone. We welcome donations, volunteers, and of course, shoppers.

Annual Live and Silent Auction
and Banquet

Every April, on the last Saturday of the month, we host this event; we just held our 12th auction.

The catered event is attended by 160 – 200 people. We have about 200 items and gift certificates to auction off. Last year was the best fundraiser so far, with about $20,000 coming in.

We accept donations of items all year, which we store until auction time. New items, antiques, vehicles that run, crafts/artwork—all are welcome. And gift certificates or gift cards for shopping, services, and restaurants in the mid-Kansas area are also welcome, with the expiration date carefully considered in light of the date of our event. You may take these donations to Grand Staff Thrift Boutique, 215 North Main, Buhler, KS, or mail/ship to GSM, 406 West A Avenue, Buhler, KS 67522.

Besides what is donated to be auctioned off, we also have several corporate sponsors who give financially to offset the expenses of the event.

We're incredibly grateful to all the businesses and individuals who donate to this fundraiser every year, the auctioneers and volunteers who donate their services, and the attendees who bid and give so generously.

The Kansas State Fair

Our first fair booth was last year in September of 2017. We sold our coffee from South Africa, items crafted in Swaziland, and ministry t-shirts designed to give our supporters a conversation starter.

We didn't make much of a profit after expenses, but we did get to spread the word about the thrift boutique, which was our primary purpose. We were happy that many of the folks who stopped by the booth also came to the thrift boutique in the weeks following the fair.

Hopefully this year, people who loved the coffee and other items for sale will come back to find us. And since it's said that people need to hear and see something seven times for it to stick in their minds, it should also serve as another reminder to everyone that we have the store, and the reason it exists—to care for our precious Swazi children.

Child Sponsorship

This part of the ministry has been in place for twelve years. We've had over 200 children go through our sponsorship program, which in most cases also meant they got one meal every school day. This has typically required $25 per month for an elementary-aged child, and $50 per month for high schoolers. But high school fees have increased, and in most cases, we need to come up with additional funds to cover the expenses.

We're gradually phasing out sponsorship in Manzini, Bhunya, Mangcongco, and Luhlokohla. We won't abandon the children who are already sponsored; we'll continue to help them until they complete high school. And if their sponsors choose to pay for university or trade school, we will also facilitate that.

But as I mentioned earlier, to have excellent outcomes in the lives of our sponsored children, they need four areas functioning well: home, church, school, and the funds and relationships GSM provides. The children in these four churches are scattered over a distance, which creates challenges in our oversight and ministry.

Our ministry partners have to take public transportation when they visit the children's homesteads, churches, and schools. They do their best to follow up when a child has difficult changes at home. They try to find out why a child is missing church. They talk to the teachers about low grades and do their best to provide some tutoring for the kids who are struggling in school.

But we're unable to provide what is greatly needed: ongoing contact on a daily basis. Since many homes are without electricity, visits after dark are unproductive. And transport closes in remote areas very early. So our ministry partners might be waiting at a homestead when the child gets home from school, but there is very little time left before darkness comes or transport is over for the day.

Has sponsorship been worth it with these challenges? Definitely! The children who have been sponsored for the last twelve years have been given tools to make a better life, and eternity has been affected. We're grateful for every sponsor who made that possible.

But now that we have a site where some children can live and others from the village are within walking distance, we will have a deeper impact simply because of the easy proximity.

We can now meet daily needs by sponsoring children in various ways in the village of Sipete and on the site of the care center.

One of the needs is for individuals willing to sponsor children for the feeding program. It will cost us $10 per month to feed a child and provide the Bible lesson materials. That doesn't sound like much, but if we have 100 children to feed, that's $1,000 every month. So sponsors are important to this part of the ministry to the kids.

Children of parents who can't afford to send their children to our preschool will also need sponsors. A complete scholarship for a preschooler:

$15 per month or

$180 annually

As we continue to take in new children at the care home(s), we will also be looking for sponsors for them. Expenses vary for these children, but here is an estimate of the annual expenses, which includes doctor and dentist visits, clothing and shoes, schooling, food, and all care:

Preschool child: $2,975

Primary child: $3,100

High School child: $3,500

We realize that not everyone who is moved with compassion can afford to take on the entire sponsorship for one of these children. But it's fine to do a partial sponsorship, with each child having more than one sponsor.

(And as you'll read in the next section, we also have a huge need for people called to donate monthly or annually to offset administrative costs and the expenses of our mission trips and to help with the expenses of whatever the current building project is.)

Monthly or Annual Giving

As always, having monthly donors is a tremendous blessing to this ministry. Our trips to Swaziland are expensive, especially because of the cost of flights. I go twice a year and usually take a board member with me.

Most sponsorship nonprofits add their administrative costs into the price of sponsoring a child. There is absolutely nothing wrong with that. It's a legitimate expense, because if you can't purchase office supplies and take the trips, etc., then you can't keep the ministry afloat. The children won't have their needs met.

But we've never added any of our administrative expenses to the child sponsorship. We decided at the beginning to set sponsorship funds aside to use only on the children. It sounded noble . . . and I'm smiling while I type this. But as we've grown, the administrative expenses have also increased.

We were thinking too small. It was an easy thing to raise a small amount for administrative purposes in the beginning. We only traveled to Swaziland once every two years, and our vision was only to send children to school. I only spent a few hours every week keeping the ministry moving forward.

In those early years, when Tracy and I took mission trips, we did fundraisers such as rummage sales, dinners, and so on. We also mailed letters to individuals who might be willing to help get us to our destination with a financial contribution.

But now our schedules don't allow for that. Tracy is still working as a machinist, and I'm more than full-time as the executive director of GSM. (No, I'm not paid full-time. Smile.)

In addition, many of the people in our lives who were part of financing the trips in the early days are now sponsoring a child, helping with the fundraisers, donating monthly, or volunteering at the boutique—or all of the above. We can't ask people to do more when they're already "all in."

So that means we must raise those funds in other ways. They do have to come from somewhere.

We honestly had no idea the amazing ways the Lord would give us a dream that was so big—truly God-sized. One that we could never possibly accomplish without His provision.

And one we could never possibly accomplish without His people joining their hands with ours.

What a journey that's been! For most of my life, I've been stubbornly independent. I don't like to ask for help. I'd rather do things myself. But God's work is never meant to take place in isolation. He wants us to depend on Him, but also on each other.

His dreams are way too big for any one person, including the finances required to get the job done.

Even when we first visited Swaziland, ready to move there if that's what the Lord wanted us to do, He made it clear that He wanted us to go back home and raise funds. The pastors in Swaziland caring for the children didn't have the resources to meet the needs.

I've never minded raising funds if it's a rummage sale or dinner; I'm not afraid of hard work! But to ask people to give out of their pockets without receiving anything tangible in return? Ugh! Remember, I already told you that I'm independent? God has such a sense of humor. He wanted to strip me of self-sufficiency.

Yes, He also wanted to humble me. Not to be mean to me, but to help me grow. And to get me to a place where I could participate with Him—and His people—to accomplish the bigger picture of His dreams for the Swazi children.

In fact, He loves calling us to something that is so much bigger than us, we can never do it without His touch and His people. Because then He receives the glory, not any person.

And certainly, that is where we are as individuals, and as members of the Grand Staff Ministries team.

So my attitude about asking for financial help has changed. (Also for asking for volunteer help—the children's needs simply won't be met without many of us making sacrifices for them.)

Now it's a joy to invite others to be part of what the Lord is doing in Swaziland! I know firsthand what a blessing it is to experience what James called "pure religion that is unblemished." Taking care of the fatherless and widows in their distress is something we can do here on earth that affects eternity!

This year, besides child sponsorship, we must cover these expenses:

- Purchase food and Bible lesson supplies for the kitchen
- Pay our ministry partners in Swaziland who care for the children in the sponsorship program and will help at the feeding program and preschool as needed
- Pay our preschool teachers/aides
- Pay the day laborers who do the building projects
- Make the two mission trips (expenses for one board member and me, as others raise their own funds to go)
- Build and furnish the GSM Swazi office
- Develop the sustainability projects/agriculture
- Cover administrative costs

This year's budget, besides sponsorships, is $145,000.

So far we've raised $33,425. We can expect $2,590 yet this year from monthly donors, and the thrift boutique can be counted on for at least $20,000 by the end of December.

So we still need to raise $78,985 of non-sponsorship funds.

Every gift matters. Some of our current monthly donors send $20, $40, or $50 per month, and one has given $10 a month for several years—and that still counts! We give in light of eternity, according to the grace we've been given.

Meanwhile, I unashamedly ask you to prayerfully consider being part of the team making a difference in the lives of the

Swazi children. We're asking for 150 individuals who will commit to giving $50 - $100 per month.

I speak for the entire GSM board of directors when I thank everyone who has helped financially in the past, and also to those of you who are moved to help now. You may mail a check to:

GSM
PO Box 321
Buhler, KS 67522

You may also set up monthly donations through your online banking or request a form to have your donations automatically withdrawn.

Or you may make a one-time gift on our website's donate page at www.grandstaffministries.com/donate.php.

We are a registered 501(c)3 nonprofit organization, and we mail tax receipts in January.

If you are unable to do a monthly donation, would you consider doing a fundraiser? Maybe a rummage sale or a dinner at your church? I'm always amazed at the funds generated at a one-time event. People really do love to be part of something that is making a difference. And if you're pleased with the results, perhaps you can make it an annual event, because these types of fundraisers begin to draw a following when they're repeated. I have several pages of ideas for fund-raising events, and I'd be happy to send them to you; send request to becky@grandstaffministries.com.

You've heard me mention my friend Marlene Bagnull. She told me about reading the book *What Do You Say to a Hungry World?* by Stan Mooneyham, who was then president of World Vision. She was so moved by the book, she organized a World Hunger Bazaar. Women from seventeen churches worked for months making handcrafts that they sold at a bazaar in November. They raised almost $4,000.

If we all do what we can, using the resources God has given us, whether it's finances or time or energy or ideas, the Good Shepherd's care will reach into the lives and hearts of many more children.

Women's Events/ Churches/Conferences

I'm always grateful to the organizations and churches that invite me to share about what Grand Staff Ministries is doing in Swaziland.

Marlene Bagnull, Director of the Colorado Christian Writer's Conference and the Greater Philly Christian Writer's Conference, has become a very dear friend to me and to Grand Staff Ministries. She has graciously allowed me to share at her conferences for several years now. Even though I haven't made the trip to Philadelphia for several years, she and Barb Haley, author and also a precious friend of mine, have sometimes presented GSM's mission in my absence.

Many of our monthly sponsors of children have come from these conferences. And so have some of our generous donors. Marlene has a heart for hurting children, and she connects people beautifully to share the love of Jesus with them. Barbie is one of the most giving people I've ever known, quietly meeting needs and blessing people, just because she loves being part of what Jesus is up to. God bless you both!

The Center Church in Wichita, Kansas, a Foursquare church pastored by David and Marla Beeson, has been generously supporting our work in Swaziland for a few years now. They supplied toiletries and toys for us to take for care packages one July. They donated funds to buy goats and chickens. They've given financial donations for whatever is needed several times.

And recently they started a campaign to raise the $1,000 needed for the preschool's application to the Swazi government and tables and chairs for one classroom. Within two weeks, they'd already raised $600 of the amount needed, and the rest came in quickly after that. We're so thankful for the hearts of this couple and their congregation, and for allowing me to share regularly at their services. Thank you, friends, for being generous contributors, as well as faithful prayer partners and compassionate listeners when I need to pour out my heart.

I absolutely love speaking at women's events and conferences/retreats. That's my favorite venue—being with the Lord's gals! I've done annual conferences, Mother/Daughter events, Christmas events, and girlfriend getaways. I speak about things worth fighting for: family, marriage, wayward children, faith, and of course, our dear Swazi children. I appreciate it when the group allows me to take at least a few minutes to mention our mission and allow a response to the needs.

Besides sharing at women's events, I'm also available to do concerts in churches, share our vision for the children in Swaziland, or share on another topic and just give a quick glimpse of our mission. (We'd like to produce a 3- or 4-minute video that could be shown in churches who are willing to consider partnering with us, as well. If you're gifted in that area and would be willing to donate your services, that would be a huge blessing to the ministry.)

I also love opening our bed and breakfast for girlfriend nights. We encourage women to get a group of six to twelve women to come with their jammies—and without their stresses from life! I can provide a dessert bar and a time of worship and a short devotional. Some of the groups like for me to share briefly what we're doing in Swaziland, too. You can contact me for more information on pricing, available dates, etc., and we'll customize the evening to suit your needs. Our outside pool is open in the summer, and the fireplace in the sunroom is cozy in the winter.

Note: The bed and breakfast isn't technically part of GSM. When we opened it, we used the same name because we already had the logo, and we figured when guests asked us about the name, it would give us the opportunity to share about the ministry. That has proven true! Our thinking was also that when Tracy retired, it would give us some income that would allow us to continue to pay our bills even when we were on extended trips to Swaziland. I've asked our ministry board of directors if they would like for us to change the name of the b & b, but they are comfortable leaving it like it is. It definitely ends up being a ministry much of the time as we serve tired pastors, discouraged Christians, couples with troubled marriages, families torn apart by wayward children, and more. Then there are times when God sends someone to minister to us when we need it. We've made tremendous friends through the years, many of whom have also become sponsors of children in Swaziland. It's all connected for the Lord's Kingdom business. Hallelujah!

I also plan to host women's conferences in five to ten major cities in the USA in the future. I'm still working on the speakers and worship leaders, and I'm selecting national companies to ask for corporate sponsorships for the events. I believe there is a message God wants His "gals" to hear about being "enough." We will tie this in with the needs of our Swazi children who don't have enough, and a God who is always more than enough.

And if you are a speaker or do Christian concerts, would you please consider making GSM your featured ministry at your events? We will supply a short video and printed materials to make it easy for people to respond with donations, sponsorships, or invitations to share at their home churches or events.

Going and Doing

We take a small team with us to Swaziland twice a year, usually January and July/August. The cost to go is between $4,000 - $5,000, with January usually costing the lesser amount, because flights aren't as much at that time of year.

We are also praying for long-term missionaries to serve with Grand Staff Ministries. As I mentioned earlier, Hannah Ball is raising her funds to go, but we won't allow her to go alone. We really need a couple to help oversee the ministry and give direction to the efforts. But we would also love to have other women join the team. Teachers, principals, preachers, administrators, and all lovers of children—we have work for you in Swaziland. Minimum two-year term.

We also need someone good at organization and secretarial skills to help locally in our Buhler, Kansas office at least one day at week, and preferably even more. Filing, answering emails, making phone calls, updating the website, keeping me on track (yes, that would be a task!)—are all needed. At this point, we are looking for a volunteer to fill this important position.

Thank you for prayerfully considering being part of the Grand Staff Ministries team to share the love of our Savior with the children of Swaziland. Together, we will give them hope and help keep their dreams alive. God bless you!

Music to My Ears

Sweat glistens on Sibusiso's forehead as he bends down to pull fresh lettuce leaves from the garden at Shepherd's Care Home. He runs his fingers through the rich soil, and it is dark under his nails. His thoughts turn to wonder. How does a tiny seed grow into nourishment for an entire family? Sibusiso pauses and turns his eyes to the blue sky, marveling at the Creator. He whispers his thanks.

Gardening is hard work in the hot sun, but a wide grin splits his face when he hears the children's chatter when they arrive home from school. The security guard unlocks the gate for them, and they continue up the dirt path to the front door. Their voices fade.

Memories flood Sibusiso's mind. He compares their childhood experiences with his own. He spent days in hunger, stayed alone in his room on holidays, and fed his anger at the world that kept turning, even when he couldn't find his place to belong in it.

He shakes his head and wipes an escaped tear on his checkered sleeve, grateful that these kids have found a home early in life.

He decides his basket is full enough, and he heaves it up, feeling the ripple of the muscles he's developed since starting his work as a gardener and handyman on the site.

His smile returns when he enters the house, because the kids tackle him with hugs, all talking at once about their day. He nearly drops the produce.

But he sets the basket on the kitchen counter and greets Siza. Contentment warms his heart. He knows Patrick will come down to the house soon, calling it a day on the preschool building and sending the laborers on their way. The two men will embrace and pound each other's backs, greeting each other with loud hellos and reporting on the progress they've made.

The smell of a chicken stew boiling on the stove makes Sibusiso's stomach growl, and he knows that Siza will be quick to invite him to stay for supper. He's eager to share the Scripture he read that morning, curious to hear what Patrick has been reading, and especially happy as he anticipates the stories the children will tell about the antics of their classmates that day.

Tears come back to Sibusiso's eyes as he moves to the sink to wash his hands. But this time they are happy tears filling his eyes the same way love is filling his heart.

After all the rejection he suffered, after disappointment chased away his hopes for a good future, his blessings now outweigh his sorrows. He is known. He's loved. He knows his place.

He is finally at home.

Jesus is playing a beautiful song with this once-bruised reed. Sibusiso, one of our Men of Courage, is only one of many whose lives have been changed by love.

My heart fills like his does, gratitude and joy making a melody of adoration to our King.

Thank you for making music with us.

"If You Could See Them Like I See Them"

© 2010 Becky Spencer

Another sea of faces in a third world house of hope,
Lost in my embraces, clinging children try to cope.
Bloated bellies, tattered clothes—their tragic tales unfold.
Fearful eyes reveal the stories words have never told.

The needs are overwhelming, my meager gifts too few,
My grandeur plans defective; there is far too much to do.
My heart sinks, 'cause I know my work will barely make a dent,
Until my Savior tells me, "That is not why you were sent.

"If you could see them like I see them,
You'd see all I dreamed they would be.
You'd see the gifts I placed inside,
You'd understand My sense of pride,
And all the joy they give to Me.

"If you could see them like I see them,
You'd love one of them in My Name.
You'd give your life just to free them,
Imagine how it feels to be them,
If you could see them like I see them."

I glanced once more around me, and I saw with different eyes.
Renewed compassion found me as I listened to their cries.
Smiling now, I stop to pick up some lost mother's son.
I knew I couldn't save them all, but I could help this one.

"If you could see them like I see them,
You'd see all I dreamed they would be.
You'd see the gifts I placed inside,
You'd understand My sense of pride,
And all the joy they give to Me.

"If you could see them like I see them,
You'd love one of them in My Name.

242

You'd give your life just to free them,
Imagine how it feels to be them,
If you could see them like I see them."

Heaven weeps as their cries pierce the night;
I call, "Don't just hear, but do.
For in My love, I see their hearts
The same way I see you."

"Can You Save Me?"

© 2012 Anna (Spencer) Harper

Your brown eyes are the highlight, starlight
Of my miserable, selfish life.
I see you workin' hard every day
Just to keep a little bit of food on your plate.

You help your sister and she loves you;
You're hopin' that someday she could go to school.
You ask God, "Why am I this way?
Why can't you come down and save me?"

God told me to fly across the ocean
Just to find that one little boy.
A boy who asked,
"God, can You save me?"

Why do we question God's Holy Word
When He told us to go into all the world?
When we should really be askin' Him
If we have enough true passion.

It's time to give our hearts,
Bring light into the dark.
And when we trust in You
We know that You'll come through.

Suggested Reading List

When Helping Hurts. Steve Corbett and Brian Fikkert. Chicago: Moody Publishers, 2009

Kisses from Katie. Katie Davis with Beth Clark. New York: Howard Books, 2011

Scared. Tom Davis. Colorado Springs: David C. Cook, 2009

Foreign to Familiar: A Guide to Understanding Hot – and Cold – Climate Cultures. Sarah Lanier. Hagerstown MD: McDougal Publishing, 2000

Ministering Cross-Culturally: An Incarnational Model for Personal Relationships. Sherwin Lingenfelter and Marvin Mayers. Grand Rapids: Baker Academic, 2016

Toxic Charity. Robert D. Lupton. New York: HarperCollins, 2011

What Do You Say to a Hungry World? Stan Mooneyham. Waco TX. Word Books, 1977

Radical. David Platt. Colorado Springs: Multnomah Books, 2010

Radical Together. David Platt. Colorado Springs: Multnomah Books, 2011

Follow Me. David Platt. Carol Stream, IL: Tyndale House 2013

He Walks Among Us. Richard and Renee Stearns. Nashville: Thomas Nelson, 2013

Unfinished. Richard Stearns. Nashville: Thomas Nelson, 2013

The Hole in Our Gospel. Richard Stearns. Nashville: W Publishing/ Thomas Nelson, 2014

Watch for the next book in the Worth Fighting For Series:

Book 2: Faith Is Not a Garden Hose
(It's a white-water rapids ride on the river of God's will!)

About the Author

Becky and her husband Tracy have been married for forty-two years. They raised eight children—four birth and four adopted—and so far, they have twenty-seven grandchildren.

When she's not traveling, Becky stays busy running Grand Staff Bed and Breakfast; serving vulnerable children in Swaziland, Africa; directing Grand Staff Ministries; finding treasures, volunteering at Grand Staff Thrift Boutique; and enjoying her role as Grammy.

She doesn't go looking for a fight, but battles find her. So "The Fight Lady" writes, sings, and speaks about things worth fighting for: family, marriage, wayward children, faith, adoption, and her dear Swazi children.

You'll find Becky and Tracy fighting the good fight of faith in Buhler, Kansas.

To order additional copies of *A Bruised Reed* or to schedule Becky to speak or sing at your event, please contact her at: becky@grandstaffministries.com

  1 copy: $14.95 plus tax and shipping
 10 copies: $12.95 each plus tax and shipping
    (If mailed to the same address)

Becky Spencer, 406 West A, Buhler, KS 67522
www.grandstaffministries.com
www.grandstaffbedandbreakfast.com

GALLERY

Becky's mama, Pattie Belden,
with the gogos in Mangcongo

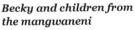

Sponsored children
receiving backpacks
with toys

Becky and children from
the mangwaneni

Shepherd's Care Family, August 2018

Children praying together

Jana Durham loving on a a couple of Swazi kids

Back: Siza, Menzie, Dana Siscoe, Steve Rees, Colani, Tracy Front: Patrick and Matsebula children

Tracy— digging the foundation for the care home

Becky's daughter, Sara Nowlan, holding a Swazi girl,

Josh Martinson with his sponsored child, Bezwe

Linda Basler snuggling a Swazi baby

Children from Mangcongo singing for us

Children on the mangwaneni

Becky, Sara Nowlan, and Jubilee Yocum singing at the mangwaneni

Playing hula hoops at the weiner roast at Bunya

Typical meal served after church

Sara with a mama in Mangcongo

Jubilee Yocum chatting with Pastor Sambo as a child from church plays between them

*Tracy and Becky
with the children from
Mangcongo*

Janie Ediger grinding maize

*Becky purchasing
school supplies*

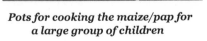

*Pots for cooking the maize/pap for
a large group of children*

A Bruised Reed

Endnotes

[1]http://www.med-health.net/Protein-Deficiency-Diseases.html Last updated on March 29, 2018

[2]http://www.chaimbentorah.com/2014/01/word-study-bruised-reed-isaiah-423-a-bruised-reed-break-smoking-flax-quench-bring-judgment-truth-beautiful-double-meaning-word-reed-qaneh-history-lesson-dav/January 13, 2014

[3]*Parables of Jesus, Part 4,* Joyce Meyer, December 7, 2017,https://sermons-online.org/joyce-meyer/parables-of-jesus-part-4-joyce-meyer

[4] Stearns, Richard, *The Hole in Our Gospel,* 198

Made in the USA
Columbia, SC
20 April 2019